Kosher Harry

Nick Grosso was born in London. In 1993 his monologue
Mama Don't was produced at the Royal Court Young
People's Theatre. The following year his first stage play,
Peaches was produced by the Royal Court in association with
the Royal National Theatre. In 1995 and 1996 he was
writer in residence at the Royal National Theatre Studio.
His second stage play *Sweetheart* (1996) was produced at the
Royal Court Theatre Upstairs and toured regionaly. *Real
Classy Affair* his third stage play was produced by the Royal
Court at the Ambassadors Theatre. His work has also been
produced in Europe and the US.

Bloomsbury Methuen Drama

An imprint of Bloomsbury Publishing Plc

50 Bedford Square   1385 Broadway
London   New York
WC1B 3DP   NY 10018
UK   USA

www.bloomsbury.com

Bloomsbury is a registered trade mark of Bloomsbury Publishing Plc

First published 2002 by Methuen

© Nick Grosso 2002

Visit www.bloomsbury.com to find out more about our authors and their books You will find extracts, author interviews, author events and you can sign up for newsletters to be the first to hear about our latest releases and special offers.

British Library Cataloguing-in-Publication Data
A catalogue record for this book is available from the British Library.

ISBN: PB: 978-0-4137-7264-0
       EPDF: 978-1-4081-4991-1
       EPUB: 978-1-4081-1766-8

Library of Congress Cataloging-in-Publication Data
A catalog record for this book is available from the Library of Congress.

Kosher Harry

Nick Grosso

B L O O M S B U R Y

LONDON • NEW DELHI • NEW YORK • SYDNEY

To my beautiful sweet dad.
May you rest in peace.
We love you very much.

Kosher Harry premiered at the Royal Court Theatre, London, on 18 April 2002. The cast was as follows:

Waitress	Claudie Blakley
Man	Martin Freeman
Cabbie	Mark Benton
Old Woman	June Watson

Director Kathy Burke
Designer David Roger
Lighting Designer Colin Granfell
Sound Designer Scott George

Part One

North-west London. Kosher Harry. Signed photographs of stars of a bygone age adorn the walls of the Jewish diner.

A scruffy **Man** *with his shirt untucked enters. He is wet and dishevelled as there is a storm outside. Only the table by the door is free. A waitress in spectacles and uniform walks on and watches man who is oblivious to her presence. She clearly likes what she sees.* **Man** *looks towards someone off stage who indicates he can sit. He smiles back and does so. A* **Waitress** *walks up to him and wipes the table clean.*

Waitress   i'm sorry sir you can't sit there

Man   what

Man *watches* **Waitress** *walk off. He is unsure whether to remain seated.* **Waitress** *walks back on with menus and glasses and napkins and cutlery.*

Waitress   people coming

Man   oh i see

Waitress (*lays the table*)   a table will be free in a minute

Man   yeh fine i don't mind whatever

Waitress   i hope that's okay

Man   that's great it's just that waitress over there . . .

Waitress   what the russian one

Man   i dunno where she's from i didn't get the chance to . . .

Waitress   i think you mean the russian one sir

Man   yeh the russian one

Waitress   gladiola

Man   gladi what what

Waitress   well that's what *we* call her anyway she's new she doesn't understand the rules

Man   she said i could sit down but i don't mind really i'll sit anywhere whatever suits you

Waitress   she hasn't quite got used to it but she will eventually

Man   i don't think she saw the others

Waitress   well it's not her section you see sir

Man   i see

Waitress   and she should know that really

Man   should she

Waitress   seeing as *that* section over there's hers

Man   that one

Waitress   yeh the one where i don't go

Man   oh

Waitress   so you'd have thought it was obvious but it's not you see sir no not to her she seems to think well i dunno what she thinks she must think i act this way for some reason other than: them's the rules (*gapes at* **Man**.) it's not just odd sir

Man   is it not no

Waitress   no it's incredible *mind*boggling even

Man   perhaps she needs the tips perhaps there's no *sections* in russia

Waitress (*stares at man and nods uncertainly*)   yeh maybe that's it

Man   the eastern bloc after all you have to bear in mind where she comes from i mean it must be hard to adjust to our habits

Waitress   like sections you mean sir

Man   sections

(*nods*)

elections

Waitress   erections

Man (*checks*)   –*civilisation* – everything – we're poles apart

Man (*stares at* **Waitress** *nonplussed*)   different nations nearly

Waitress   clearly

Man   it must be strange

Waitress   ohh damn right it is

Man   i mean we're *foreigners* to her

Waitress   what

Man   i'm just saying (*He taps his temple.*) have a think

Waitress   yeh you may be right

Man   *we're* the aliens in her book

Waitress   what

Man   she probably rings home every night and laughs about us – laughs at our little ways

Waitress   you reckon

Man   oh yeh *definitely* – well not *mine* obviously – yours

Waitress   what

Man   well she doesn't know me does she she doesn't *know* my little ways

Waitress   you mean she laughs about *me*

Man (*nods*)   she probably rings her sister in moscow or wherever and they titter at your expense

Waitress   you reckon

Man   oh yeh *regularly*

Waitress   the sneaky *bitch*

Man   her in london she in moscow all they do is gossip about *you*

Waitress (*stares back at* **Man**)   i bet she has cable

Man   what

Waitress   cheap international calls

Man   they probably stay up all night *wetting* themselves over these section thingies you keep harping on about

Waitress (*shouts over at* **Russian**)   well i didn't bleeding *invent* em

Man   sections all she talks about is sections she's got sections on the *brain* . . . (**Waitress** *glares at* **Man**.) *they* say

Waitress (*shouts over at* **Russian**)   i just *work* here thank you

Man   laughing at your pigtails i bet they do

Waitress (*turns towards* **Man**)   what

Man   the way you wear your hair

Waitress   what *about* it

Man   i bet they have a *right* ol laugh

Waitress (*glares at* **Man**)   are you being rude

Man   nah not *me* sweetheart – *her* – it's *her* over *there* look

Waitress   what

Man   well have a look i mean she even mimics your *walk*

Waitress (*looks perplexed*)   does she (*looks over at* **Russian**.) nah she don't

Man   well it's a bit wonky

Waitress (*titters*)   yeh so it is (*She glares at* **Man**.) oi i walk just *fine* thank you

Man   tell *her* she's the one (*He shouts over at* **Russian**.) oi get it right lovely

Waitress (*looks ōver at* **Russian**)   well *she* can tease i mean if she undid her shirt any more there'd be an avalanche an avalanche of russian boobs they'd have to hire a crane to hike em up again

Man (*draws his breath sharply*)   cutting

Waitress   well look at her (*She sneers disparagingly.*) what a state

Man   i think it's great (**Waitress** *looks at* **Man** *surprised.*) the carefreeness

Waitress   it's a shocking scandal

Man   the continental abandon

Waitress   she wants a man that's what it is sir they come here they get all *brassed* up and then they snare one *so* simple even *they* can keep him (**Man** *gawps at* **Waitress**.) it's entirely true

Man (*points towards* **Russian**'s *section*)   can i sit *there*

Waitress   i'll tell you something shall i sir (*She sizes up* **Man** *who looks back intrigued.*) let you in on a little secret

Man   go on darling

Waitress   a little background to my brevity

Man   hit me baby

Waitress   the previous one what worked here before

Man   oh yeh

Waitress   gladiola

Man (*looks shocked*)   another one

Waitress   well i *called* her gladiola i mean her real name was bratislavan or something i mean *i* couldn't say it i can hardly say brata bleeding *slava*

Man   tricky

Waitress   exactly

Man   what a palaver

Waitress   anyway i sorta looked after her sir

Man   ahh

Waitress   well i mean she was from brata bleeding bloody *slava* poor cow she hadn't even seen running *water*

Man   no

Waitress   let alone civil sorts in suits like those what come here (*She sneers at* **Man**.) present company excepted

Man (*looks affronted*)   oi these are da boomest rags darling

Waitress   are they really

Man   they don't look it

Waitress   no i noticed

Man   but that's bcos it's not au fait in higher circles to flaunt one's impeccable credentials

Waitress   i see

Man   you see

Waitress   enlightening

Man   precisely and you should know that working around here

Waitress   why

Man   what (*They stare at each other.*) st john's wood

Waitress   so

Man   you know that paul mccartney

Waitress (*looks perplexed*)   the beatle

Man   well he lives around here

Waitress (*scoffs*)   yeh when he's not in *scotland* or wotnot

Man   well obviously he's a busy man i mean he can't reside in one place

Waitress   why not

Man   he has to show his *face* darling

Waitress   evade tax you mean

Man (*scoffs*)   no no not our paul he's a beatle he's english . . .

Waitress   so

Man   he likes *football* (*He shakes his head incredulously.*)

Waitress   what about him anyway

Man   well you know his youngest

Waitress   stella

Man   mary

Waitress   the fashion guru

Man   that's stella

Waitress   i know

Man   well she went to my school

Waitress   where

Man   just around the corner here

Waitress   happy times was they sir

Man (*checks*)   what

Waitress   well

Man (*stares back at* **Waitress** *nonplussed*)   i was fine at school thanks for asking

Waitress   no i thought you may have been a tad unpopular

Man (*scoffs dismissively*)   why would you

Waitress   bcos you're on your own sir

Man   i like dining alone so what

Waitress   so she went there so what then this stella then

Man   mary

Waitress   that's the one

Man   well her dad coulda sent her anywhere

Waitress   cheapskate

Man   what

Waitress   so he lumbered the state

Man (*tuts dismissively*)   no no you don't get it

Waitress   i bet she got free dinners

Man   those who have: *disguise* the fact darling: it's an english trait

Waitress   and that's why you dress down (*She indicates clothes of* **Man** *who feigns modesty.*)

Man   well i couldn't *say* could i i'd be breaking a code

Waitress   i'll have to make my own assumption

Man   you shall

Waitress   i'll assume you're a tatty bastard

Man (*looks pleasantly surprised*)   fine

Waitress   and that's why she's so common

Man   who

Waitress   ol stella

Man   what

Waitress   bcos she went to a slagheap school

Man (*nods pensively*)   perhaps

Waitress (*shakes her head disdainfully*)   loose as anything they are them lot i bet she breezed into your school and wiggled her hips and whisked all you starstruck brittle boys off your feet sir

Man   no no not at *all*

Waitress   flounced into school like she was something special did she sir all dolled up and pouting

Man   er . . .

Waitress   *well*

Man   she was only *eight*

Waitress   conniving *whore*

Man   so . . . (*He stares nonplussed at* **Waitress** *who composes herself once again.*)

Waitress   oh yeh

Man   gladiola the first

Waitress   well she was working here although none too cleverly but i covered for her of course i regret it now

Man   why

Waitress   well i was seeing the chef at the time

Man   oh yeh

Waitress   this 'antonio' (*She checks.*) why am i telling you this

Man   bcos you're bored

Waitress   i have work to do

Man   then do it

Waitress   i'll get in trouble you don't realise

Man   then fuck off

Waitress   no no my shift hasn't started

Man   what

Waitress   not properly

Man   when does it

The storm grows fiercer outside. **Waitress** *shouts over towards* **Russian**.

Waitress   gladiola will you cover for me darling i'm taking a break (*She pulls out a chair and sits.*)

Man   can you do that

Waitress   she dunno the difference she works my section anyway . . .

Man   poor thing

Waitress   i may as well get something from it

Man   so you was seeing the chef

Waitress   oh yeh (*She nods.*) 'antonio'

Man   spanish

Waitress   yeh but pleasant with it

Man   so what happened

Waitress   and you know what they say about latins sir

Man   er – no no

Waitress   their bedside manner

Man   oh yeh

Waitress   'animals'

Man   so i've heard

Waitress   no it's *all* true

Man   i'm thrilled for you

Waitress   well it was *well* clear ol bratislava had the hots for him but it was *also* clear that while he was with me he wouldn't even *notice* her i mean . . . (*She shows herself off.*) why should he

Man   no

Waitress   i mean let's not be *coy*

Man   no

Waitress   i mean this was before i had stopped *not* smoking so my skin was clear and these bags you see here . . .

Man   where

Waitress   just *there* look (*She lifts her spectacles a moment so* **Man** *can see the bags under her eyes.*)

Man   oh yeh

Waitress   'non fucking existent'

Man (*looks impressed*)   really

Waitress   also i was getting plenty of exercise on account of his high testosterone so i was in good shape i mean i looked fucking great and i had a smile as big as *china* i mean i looked like a fucking smiling *chinaman* half the time . . .

Man   charming

Waitress   and my hair was all different it was like . . .

Man   good good

Waitress (*checks*)   what

Man   what

Waitress   what *about* my hair

Man   nothing

Waitress   i *have* to wear it like this

Man   i know

Waitress   this is a fucking *diner* you know not a flaming *nightclub*

Man   so what did this gladiola do da do what what

Waitress   what

Man   well

They stare at each other.

Waitress   she waited

Man   until

Waitress   we split up

Man   when was that

Waitress   conniving *bitch*

Man   when was *that*

Waitress   oh soon after (*She composes herself again.*)

Man   why

Waitress   well he was bothering me

Man   how come

Waitress   well he had these spanish habits i can't go into sir

Man   i see

Waitress   greasy spanish monkey he was sir but sexy with it but sex isn't everything although having said that when he cooked his chihuahua in the bedroom i wouldn't *necessarily* have agreed with you

Man   no

Waitress   anyway we became good friends rather than lovers although friends who loved each other . . .

Man   yeh i know

Waitress   exactly yeh then one day he invited me to spain

Man (*raises his eyebrows*)   oh *did* he now

Waitress (*slaps* **Man** *playfully*)   no no it was nothing like *that* sir he'd bought this ruin and he needed *help*

Man   what sorta ruin

Waitress   oh just a pile of rubble in the desert it was *awful* well it was okay i suppose apart from i invited gladiola

Man   what the *fuck* . . .

Waitress   well she was a mate don't forget and he had his friends there and i didn't wanna hang on his *coat* tails all the time

Man   i see

Waitress   anyway tony

Man   tony

Waitress   antonio

Man   i see

Waitress   and his mates drove there while me and gladys . . .

Man   gladys

Waitress   that's what i called her

Man   mad gladys

Waitress   we followed on the plane

Man   nice

Waitress   well not exactly no

Man   oh

Waitress   well gladys was acting up

Man   how

Waitress   well she wore all this make up

Man   so

Waitress (*smirks to herself*)   ugly pig needed *more* than make up i tell ya she needed an entire *operation*

Man   so what if she wore some

Waitress   well antonio was a *mate* don't forget sir i mean he'd seen me in the buff well of *course* he had he'd hardly seen me in anything *else* (*She breaks into a fit of giggles.*)

Man   so

Waitress   so i had nothing to *hide* from him i just went as i was i mean it was a week away in the spanish plain and he paid for it *all* including our flights . . .

Man   what

Waitress (*checks*)   what

Man   even hers then

Waitress   well that's what *i* thought sir i mean he hardly fucking *knew* her

Man   well good for *him*

Waitress   well it wasn't exactly a fucking break i suppose i mean we had to work

Man   on his ruin

Waitress (*nods*)   i mean i only took a scruffy shirt not unlike *yours* in fact (**Man** *looks at his shirt.*) only cleaner (**Man**'s *face drops.*) and a pair of cut off jeans and some spare knicks i mean it was hard *graft* out there it really was and besides there was no night spots or anything and gladice knew bcos i *told* her but when she arrived . . . (*She shakes her head.*)

Man   what

Waitress   she looked like a fucking fashion shoot

Man   harpers bazaar

Waitress   exactly

Man   lip gloss

Waitress   all sorts

Man   jesus

Waitress   and i hadn't even brought a fucking *toothbrush*

Man (*winces*)   i bet you reeked

Waitress   well that was *it* you see sir the more we worked well when i say *we* i mean all of us but gladice of course she hadn't anything appropriate just a party frock and a flimsy *thong* so she spent the entire week sunning herself while the rest of us sweated and toiled and generally made ourselves undesirable while little miss senorita grew ever more bronzed and sultry and sweeter and of course antonio fell for the fucking bait i mean he was working his *nuts* off poor sod and there's nothing he likes more after a hard day's slog in the sun than a few cold 'cervezas' and an adoring preening puppy

Man (*nods concurringly*)   understandable

Waitress   well i *knew* that of course

Man   so you coulda pampered him

Waitress (*checks*)   are you kidding

Man   no

Waitress   i was one of his *workmates*

Man   so

Waitress   i had become an honorary *lad*

Man (*stares at* **Waitress**)   are you sure

Waitress   i had ceased to be a sexual entity sir

Man   you

Waitress   yeh *me* darling

Man   even with your hair not in pigtails

Waitress (*glares at* **Man**)   even his mates who were no oil paintings themselves and who musta been pretty fucking desperate failed to give me a second glance (*They shake their heads dumbfoundedly.*) ohh it was the worst week of my *entire* life

Man (*nods concurringly*)   yeh i hear ya

Waitress   hold up i haven't come to the worst

Man (*checks*)   there's worse

Waitress   ohh you dunno the *half* of it

Man   can i get a drink in here (*He picks up an empty glass and inspects it disconsolately.*)

Waitress   listen to this . . .

Man   i'm absolutely *parched*

Waitress   so this place has only one bed

Man   what

Waitress   and it's one of them four poster jobbies you know sir big enough for a fucking army

Man   except

Waitress   you guessed it

Man   antonioni

Waitress   and gladi bloody ola

Man   want it . . .

Waitress   that's right

Man   for themselves

Waitress   that's right

Man   so what did you do

Waitress   well the first night we all slept together the three of us but i was *so* unwelcome

Man   how could you tell

Waitress   well things was going on

Man   what things

Waitress   well i daren't *look*

Man   how did they sound

Waitress (*stares back at* **Man**)   fun

Man   i see

Waitress   so i slept outside after that

Man (*looks shocked*)   outdoors you mean

Waitress   i told you this was a *shack* sir

Man   yeh a *love* shack

Waitress   with vasquez and marco

Man (*raises his eyebrows*)   mmm

Waitress   sadly not no

Man   oh

Waitress   i mean how would *you* feel stretched out on a pile of dirt in a grubby bag among all the fucking elements

Man   not good

Waitress   next to two horrible greasy spics

Man (*frowns disapprovingly*)   no not for me

Waitress   snorting and farting their way to sleep (**Man** *winces.*) and to cap it *all* . . .

Man   what

Waitress   they don't even fucking *fancy* me i mean how insulting is that

Man (*stares at* **Waitress** *nonplussed*)   plenty

Waitress   and all the while of course amorous sounds are emanating from . . .

Man (*raises his eyebrows*)   you know where

Waitress   exactly

Man   you know *whom*

Waitress   precisely

Man   embarrassing

Waitress   and ever so slightly annoying

Man (*shakes his head*)   you musta been well upset

Waitress   ooh i was sir

Man   i mean your beloved antonioni

Waitress (*checks*)   what (**Man** *looks stumped. She laughs to herself.*) oh *no* it wasn't that sir

Man   what

Waitress   oh no i was well over him

Man (*nods ironically*)   of course you was darling

Waitress   there was no flame flickering *there* mate

Man   so what was it

Waitress   well it was *her* of course

Man   yeh but he was *single*

Waitress (*looks bemused*)   so

Man (*looks bemused*)   what

Waitress (*chuckles to herself incredulously*)   you men are so simple minded it's *incredible*

Man   why

Waitress   well you only fall out over *tangible* things

Man   and women

Waitress (*smirks*)   women contort things much more cleverly sir it's *far* more rewarding

Man   so how did you resolve it

Waitress (*gapes at* **Man**)   are you *mad*

Man   but i thought that's what women do

Waitress   i gave her a piece of my mind

Man   where

Waitress   on the plane sir i told her *exactly* what i thought of her (**Man** *winces.*) not nice

Man   and

Waitress   guess (**Man** *looks clueless.*) she cried

Man   oh i see

Waitress   she bawled her fucking eyes out in front of everyone the stewards and everything everyone thought i was a right ol cunt (*She gapes back at* **Man**.) me (*She gapes back at* **Man**.) the fucking *innocent* (*She gapes back at* **Man**.) the fucking *put* upon (*She gapes back at* **Man**.) the one who had slogged her *arse* off all week so she could happily proffer *hers*

Man   what did she say

Waitress   well after she had been tended to by about a *million* fucking air hostesses and been given about a *billion* boiled fucking sweets she said she was unconscious

Man (*looks shocked*)   she went into a coma

Waitress (*checks*)   no no you *fool* she claimed she was un*witting*

Man   ohh

Waitress   i was mad over nothing she said sir can you *believe* that of course we never spoke after . . .

Man   no

Waitress   no of course not sir until one night she had the *nerve* to phone at three in the fucking morning

Man   to say what

Waitress   i had to climb all down the fucking *stairs* in the middle of the night and *everything*

Man   *and*

Waitress (*checks and stares back at* **Man**)   well she's been speaking to her therapist

Man   what

Waitress   oh they all need therapy

Man   who do

Waitress   bratislavan bitches

Man   and

Waitress   she just *has* to tell me sir

Man   tell you what

Waitress   i mean it's all snuck into *place* now hasn't it

Man   what has

Waitress   it's clear to anyone with half a fucking *brain*

Man   *what* is

Waitress (*nods*)   *i'm* fucked up (*She gapes back at* **Man**.) and *she's* normal (*She nods at* **Man**.) *good* therapist (*She gapes back at* **Man**.) i have some issues i should deal with (*She nods at* **Man**.) *good* fucking therapist (*She gapes back at* **Man**.) she's as right as rain (*She gapes back at* **Man**.) fucking genius or what (*She stands.*) so are you still keen on that one's continental ways (*She indicates* **Russian** *off stage.*)

Man oh the russian (*He admires **Russian** and nods gleefully.*) mmm (**Waitress** *tenses.*) well i'm lonely you said yourself a man shouldn't be alone (**Waitress** *scoffs.*) what

Waitress more handsome than venice you

Man (*looks surprised*) you reckon

Waitress more popular than margate

Man says who

Waitress go on

Man margate in winter maybe

Waitress (*scoffs*) fuck off

Man oi do they let you chat to punters like that

Waitress you're no punter fuck off

Man oh no

Waitress you'll probably sit there all day taking up space drinking a solitary sorry cup of coffee

Man decaff

Waitress of course

Man on the double make it snappy

Waitress fuck off

Man i'm flaming *parched* over here

Waitress fuck off

Man fine (*motions to rise.*)

Waitress (*raises her short skirt to reveal her thigh and releases a small note pad from inside a garter strap then a pencil from behind her ear*) so what's it to be 'happy'

Man (*gawps at waitress*) yeh you can call me happy

Waitress i just did 'miserable'

Man   okay 'bitter'

They stare at each other intently.

Waitress   well

The storm grows fiercer outside. A man with a taxi badge around his neck pushes in an elegant and conservatively dressed **Old Woman** *in a wheelchair. They are both soaked.* **Waitress** *puts her pencil back behind her ear and snaps her pad back inside her garter strap and holds the door open for them.*

Old Woman   oh thank you thank you

Cabbie   no no you're alright missus go on

Waitress   oh hello mrs cider

Old Woman   oh hello angel

Waitress (*looks towards another table off stage*)   i'm afraid your table's not quite ready

Old Woman   what was that

Waitress   your table i said

Old Woman   not ready

Cabbie   no they haven't finished building it

Old Woman   what

Cabbie (*roars with laughter*)   deaf as a llama in pyjamas

Old Woman   what

Cabbie   i was just saying

Old Woman   but it's three o'clock i make it what time is it

Cabbie   three o'clock darling two minutes

Waitress   i know mrs cider we'll soon be . . .

Old Woman   what's the matter

Waitress   oh nothing there's people there but they'll soon be . . .

Cabbie   i'll have a word . . .

Waitress   no no they're almost done

Old Woman   what did she say

Cabbie   she said they have a *gun* missus

Waitress   what

Cabbie   palestine terrorists

Old Woman (*looks shocked*)   in kosher harrys

Cabbie   best place for em i reckon blimey can you imagine (*He roars with laughter.*)

Old Woman   where are they

Waitress   oh don't listen mrs cider

Old Woman (*slaps* **Cabbie** *playfully*)   oh you're having me on

Waitress   everyone's fine

Old Woman   what did she say

Cabbie   she said have some *wine*

Waitress   i did not

Cabbie   on the house while you're waiting

Old Woman   but i don't drink

Cabbie   i'll have a brandy darling (*He licks his lips.*) lovely

Old Woman   she *knows* i don't drink

Waitress   and *you're* driving

Cabbie (*breaks into a smile*)   very well i'll have a lager (**Waitress** *walks off.* **Cabbie** *calls after her.*) and treat yourself

Old Woman   well do they want me to stay

Man   have a seat mrs – cider was it (*He gets up and pulls out a chair to make room for* **Old Woman**.)

Old Woman   oh do you mind

Cabbie *pushes* **Old Woman** *violently up to the table and pulls off her jacket and hangs it on the back of her wheelchair.*

Man   no no not at all

Cabbie   not at all missus go on (*He pulls off his jacket and also hangs it on the back of the wheelchair then pulls out a chair and sits.*) i tell you what if i wasn't working mate

Man   what

Cabbie   i'd give that waitress some lollipop

Man   hey

Cabbie   something to remember me by i mean the peccadilloes on her blimey and that other one (**Man** *looks round.*) look

Man   gladiola

Cabbie   gladi what what was it

Man   russian

Cabbie   no (*He looks surprised.*) really (**Man** *nods.*) blimey have they not got bras

Old Woman   when my husband was here

Man *and* **Cabbie** *turn and stare at* **Old Woman**.

Man   oh yeh

Cabbie   oh here we go don't get on to her bleeding husband . . .

Old Woman   we'd throw some parties

Man   oh *would* you darling

Cabbie   deaf as a blooming dodo she is

Old Woman   they'd all come

Man   who would darling

Cabbie   no no don't *encourage* her . . .

Old Woman   stars

Cabbie   reckons she was in show business

Old Woman   the old lot

Cabbie   i mean can you imagine

Man   what

Cabbie   *her* in show business

Man   and why not

Cabbie (*scoffs*)   well look at her she's ninety *two*

Man   so

Cabbie (*stares at* **Old Woman**)   nah nah (*He frowns dismissively.*) sorry (*He roars with laughter.*)

Old Woman (*looks confused*)   what's the joke

Cabbie   it ain't poss

Old Woman   what's not

Cabbie   i mean i *know* her don't forget i bring her every week don't i darling

Old Woman   what

Cabbie   here – i bring you here (**Old Woman** *stares back at* **Cabbie** *blankly.*) she's jewish

Man   so

Cabbie   well you know

Man   no

Cabbie   these jews

Man   what about em

Cabbie   think they're in show business they're just jews that's all

Old Woman   are you jewish

Cabbie   she won't pay me you know mate each week i pick her up on the dot bring her here pick her up on the dot take her home . . . (**Cabbie** *shakes his head nonplussed.*) she won't pay me

Man   why not

Cabbie   good fucking *question* mate (*He nods concurringly.*) why *not* darling (**Old Woman** *stares back at* **Cabbie** *blankly.*) *there's* a teaser

Old Woman   what was that

Cabbie   you see she can't hear

Man   you don't charge her

Cabbie   well i don't *not* charge her no i just don't broach the blooming *subject*

Man   why not

Cabbie   i mean can you imagine

Man   what

Cabbie (*lowers his voice*)   too touchy by far

Man   she's poor

Cabbie   what (*He roars with laughter.*) are you *kidding* (*He roars with laughter.*) poor – *her* (*He roars with laughter.*) blimey you should see where she lives

Man   where

Cabbie   just around the corner here

Man   st john's wood

Cabbie   well where *else* would she blooming live

Man   i dunno

Cabbie   she has one of these flash flats overlooking lords

Man   all mod cons

Cabbie   you could be *dead* in one of those and still be content (*He indicates* **Old Woman**.) blimey here's the proof

Man   so why do it

Cabbie   well she's old have a look . . .

Man   it's just a short stop

Cabbie   that's it

Man   she lives up the road

Cabbie   i can ask for two quid

Man   i suppose

Cabbie   she pretends she's deaf

Man   pretends

Cabbie   you can *hear* can't you dear

Old Woman   what

Cabbie   you see

Man   i'm not so sure

Cabbie   take my word

Man   she's good at it

Cabbie   i repeat myself and by the time she twigs and digs in her purse and counts all her fucking change i've lost a fare to mayfair or somewhere i mean it's business innit that's all it blooming is

Man   i see

Cabbie   i mean i make more by *not* charging her

Man   i see

Cabbie   in fact *she* says she's doing me a frigging *favour* . . .

Old Woman   that's *right*

Cabbie   that's how their *minds* work you see mate (*He taps his temple.*) clever people

Old Woman (*gasps*)   the best

Cabbie   not like us

Old Woman (*scoffs*)   nowhere *near*

Cabbie   i mean look *around* (*He looks around the bar.*) here's the proof (**Man** *looks around the bar.*) where are ya (**Man** *stares back at* **Cabbie** *blankly.*) hey

Man   i'm here

Cabbie   yeh i know

Man   so

Cabbie   here *where* though

Man   kosher harrys

Cabbie   aah you see

Man   what

Cabbie   have you seen the prices

Man   not lately no

Cabbie   you should check matey

Man   dear are they

Cabbie   not blooming cheap

Man   i haven't been here in ages

Cabbie   yeh you look it mate (*He sneers at* **Man** *who looks down at his attire.*) jews you see mate (*He points all around him.*) everywhere (*He points at* **Man**.) *you* could be one . . .

Man   i am

Cabbie   and it wouldn't surprise me (*He checks and stares back at* **Man**.) what

Old Woman (*her eyes light up*)   oh *are* you darling

Cabbie   well then you *know*

Man   know what

Cabbie   blooming heck i dunno why i'm telling you this you're even *more* an expert on the subject than *me* (*He chortles to himself.*) blimey (*He shakes his head to himself dumbfoundedly.*) so there you are she comes here for free don't you dear

Old Woman (*stares back at* **Cabbie** *blankly*)   what was that

Cabbie   you see she can't hear

Man   did you get that love

Cabbie   no no she's a clever ol rat she gets everything

Man   i doubt it somehow

Cabbie   oh know her well do you mate

Man   no

Cabbie   well then shut up bcos i *do* don't forget

Man   yeh but . . .

Cabbie   but fucking nothing (**Man** *stares back at* **Cabbie** *impassively.*) she's a piece of *shit*

Old Woman   oh do you mind

Man   what was that darling

Old Woman   me being here

Cabbie   no no you're *fine* lovely

Old Woman   oh you're very kind

Cabbie   think nothing of it he's proud to have us

Old Woman   i don't understand it i come every week

Cabbie (*checks*)   yeh we *know* you do darling

Old Woman   and my table's always ready

Man   are you getting hungry

Old Woman   what

Man   do you want some bread

Cabbie   *bread* he said

Man   bread

Cabbie   pretzels or something

Man   something kosher

Cabbie   a bacon sandwich

Man   anything

Cabbie   a sock in your gob to stop you talking

Old Woman   what was that

Cabbie (*mimics* **Old Woman**)   what was that

Old Woman   sorry

Cabbie   ohh for goodness sake

Old Woman (*shakes her head disapprovingly*)   the service is terribly slow

Cabbie (*feigns shock*)   no

Old Woman (*checks*)   i said . . .

Man   he *knows* what you said angel

Cabbie   no no you calm down darling don't get so worked up blimey she'll collapse on us in a minute

Man   she's fine

Cabbie   nah she's just attention seeking (*He clocks* **Old Woman**.) you be happy angel

Old Woman   what

Cabbie   happy i said

Old Woman   happy

Cabbie   happy

Man   happy he said

Old Woman   happy

Cabbie   yeh *happy* for fuck sake (*He jolts up on his feet and yells at the top of his voice.*) be fucking *happy* (*The storm grows fiercer outside.* **Man** *and an extremely hot and bothered* **Cabbie** *see* **Waitress** *walk on holding a small can of lager and smiling at them.*) oh there you are my lovely about time i'm blooming gasping

Waitress *puts down the small can of lager which* **Cabbie** *cracks open gleefully. The others watch him gulp it down thirstily then gasp contentedly.*

Old Woman   happy

Cabbie *snarls at* **Old Woman**.

Waitress   now what does everyone want

Cabbie   i'll have another lager

Waitress   mrs cider

Old Woman   a potato latka darling

Waitress   is that all

Cabbie   blimey she'll wither away if she's not careful you should be *careful* lovely you might *die*

Waitress   no salt beef mrs cider

Cabbie   of *course* salt beef . . .

Old Woman   of *course* salt beef

Cabbie   you *see*

Old Woman   no i said i want some

Cabbie   i *know* you do missus

Old Woman   of *course* i do

Cabbie   of *course* she does

Old Woman   what's wrong with you

Cabbie   yeh what's wrong with you you dozy *cow*

Waitress   what was that (*She glares at* **Cabbie**.)

Cabbie   well you don't think i spurn my saturday afternoons bringing her here just so she can have a poxy potato *latka* do you (*He smirks to himself.*) blimey

Old Woman   what took you petal

Waitress (*grits her teeth*)   oh don't you start

Old Woman   what was that

Waitress (*turns to face* **Old Woman**)   it doesn't matter

Old Woman   we was ever so worried we thought something was broken

Cabbie *looks bemused.*

Waitress   something of mine

Old Woman   that's right

Waitress   like what

Old Woman   well a teapot say

Waitress   oh i see

Old Woman   or an *ankle* even i mean it's easily done especially in those shoes you should change em darling they make you walk a bit wonky

Man   *there* you are you see

Old Woman   it's not safe sweetie

Waitress   will everyone *please* stop gabbing on about my gait (*They all stare at* **Waitress** *who glares at them.*) *thank* you

Old Woman   it's vanity that's what it is handsome stranger

Man   what is angel

Old Woman   makes em do it

Man   do what

Old Woman   wear those heels

Waitress   oi do you *mind* . . .

Old Woman   discomfort doesn't in the slightest bother em as long as they 'think' they look nice

Waitress   oh an expert are you darling

Old Woman   i mean take a look (**Old Woman** *presents* **Waitress**.) the ear rings (**Waitress** *pulls off one of her dangling ear rings and drops it on the table.*) the lipstick

Waitress *smudges her lipstick across her face.*

Cabbie   the blooming pigtails mate

Old Woman   exactly

Cabbie   no no my daughter's the same mate

Man   is she mate

Cabbie   blimey is she (*He scoffs.*) fucking hell yeh – came up to me at fourteen – *fourteen* – said dad i want a tattoo – i said guess what darling – she said what – i said fuck off – guess how old

Waitress   fourteen

Cabbie   fourteen

Man   fucking hell

Cabbie   precisely mate

Man   fourteen

Cabbie   four fucking teen mrs cider

Old Woman   how much

Cabbie   fourteen

Old Woman   what was

Cabbie   my daughter

Old Woman   what about him

Cabbie   said all her friends had one – all her fucking friends – state school

Man   i see

Cabbie   broken homes

Man   clearly

Cabbie   i said to her mum i said we can't have this we'll have to move her

Man   absolutely

Cabbie   she didn't agree

Man   what

Cabbie   perfectly normal she said

Man   no

Cabbie   straight up

Man   your missus

Cabbie   the woman i wed

Man   fucking hell

Cabbie   perfectly fucking normal – four-fucking-teen wants a tattoo perfectly fucking normal

Waitress   i don't see the problem

Cabbie (*checks*)   er . . . (*He rolls his eyeballs skywards.*) what was that dear

Waitress   it's only a fucking tattoo

Cabbie   did you *hear* that mate (*He scoffs indignantly.*) some scrawny perverted *cunt* gets his grubby hands on my lass and *damages* her

Waitress (*scoffs*)   damages her

Cabbie   *irrevocably* yeh

Waitress   he hasn't *damaged* her you silly oaf

Cabbie   she was so *perfect* before missus so un*damaged*

Old Woman   who was

Cabbie   what

Old Woman   your son

Cabbie   no no *not* my son my little *girl*

Old Woman   oh

Cabbie   she was a *princess* missus – you *know* that – untainted by this world – untouched – un-fucking-damaged – some people would *kill* to be like her

Man   like who

Cabbie   like those that *have* been damaged

Man   oh

Cabbie   against their will – against their *power* – those who never asked for anything other than to be left alone to get on with their sodding lives . . .

Old Woman   your boy is that

Cabbie (*checks*)   no no *not* my boy i'm not *talking* about my blooming boy will you shut up about him i dunno why you keep bringing him *up*

Old Woman   i never *you* did

Waitress   i don't get it what about his boy

Old Woman   has someone other than your girl been damaged

Cabbie (*checks*)   what (*He glares at* **Old Woman**.)

Old Woman   well

Cabbie (*scoffs and opens his arms*)   well i mean *you* have for a *start* love have a *look*

Waitress   yeh what happened to you darling you never said

Cabbie (*raises his voice*)   what *happened* to you darling

Old Woman   what

Cabbie   she *asked*

Old Woman   about what

Cabbie   tell her love

Waitress   the *wheelchair* mrs cider

Old Woman (*looks nonplussed*)   yeh i know it is love

Cabbie   no no she means what *happened* . . .

Man   oh leave her alone

Cabbie   yeh leave her alone you heartless *whore* it upsets her

Waitress   then you tell me

Cabbie   no no she never divulged

Man   you mean you wasn't there

Cabbie   no no i only met her subsequently

Waitress   it may have been trauma

Cabbie   probably love

Waitress   perhaps she can't remember

Cabbie   no no she forgets a lot of things that's true (*He nods concurringly.*) like her *purse* most days (*He nods concurringly.*) no no you could be right love i reckon it was shock

Waitress   of what

Cabbie (*beckons* **Man** *closer*)   west ham winning the league in nineteen fifty six (*He roars with laughter.*) no no only kidding

Waitress   well something musta happened

Cabbie   something always fucking happens dunnit mate

Man   oh

Cabbie   something *bad* something that spoils everything i mean she's perfect . . .

Waitress   who

Cabbie   there's nothing wrong with her

Waitress   the old dear

Cabbie (*checks*)   no no not *her* . . . (*He roars with laughter.*) no my little *lad*

Man   lad

Cabbie   *lass* i mean (*He stares back at* **Man.**) tell me why the fuck must she change herself hey

Waitress   it's only a fucking tattoo

Cabbie (*smirks wryly*)   she has a hell of a lot more than that mate trust me

Man   oh

Cabbie   yeh

Man   such as

Cabbie (*stares back at* **Man**)   she got herself some ear rings just to spite me

Man   well there's nothing wrong there

Cabbie   no

Man   no

Cabbie   you should see where she puts em

Cabbie *and* **Man** *stare at each other.*

Man   oh

Cabbie   got given a bracelet (**Cabbie** *nods wearily*.) belonged to my mother – belonged to *her* mother before that – *and* before that *and* before that – guess where she wears it (**Man** *looks back at* **Cabbie** *cluelessly*.) this bracelet (**Man** *looks back at* **Cabbie** *cluelessly*.) family fucking heirloom (**Man** *looks back at* **Cabbie** *cluelessly*.) generations

Waitress   on her ankle

Cabbie   on her fucking ankle mate

Old Woman *looks shocked*.

Old Woman   he doesn't

Waitress   no i do that

Man   oh do you where

Old Woman   you can't let him

Cabbie   i can't fucking *stop* her darling

Old Woman   well he should *know*

Waitress   you can't see it i'm wearing socks

Man   well pull them off what are you *shy* all of a fucking sudden

Cabbie   she should know *what* missus

Old Woman   you mean you dunno

Cabbie *stares at* **Old Woman** *nonplussed*.

Cabbie   no

Waitress   there you are you see

She has pulled off her shoe and sock. She raises her bare foot onto **Man**'s *knee. Her short skirt rises above her thigh to again reveal her garter strap.*

Old Woman   well it means you're a *harlot* of course

They all stare at **Old Woman**.

Waitress   what

Cabbie *and an oblivious* **Old Woman** *look up at* **Waitress**
*whose solitary ear ring and smudged lipstick and short skirt and
exposed thigh and garter strap and shoe in hand and bare foot resting on*
Man*'s knee make her look like a prostitute.*

Old Woman   what was that petal

Waitress   what did you say

Old Woman   no that's okay don't you worry yourself

Cabbie   a *harlot* missus

Old Woman *nods confirmingly.*

Old Woman   a *cheap* one to boot (**Cabbie** *smiles gleefully at*
Waitress.) riddled with disease (**Cabbie***'s smile grows bigger.*)
no teeth (**Cabbie***'s smile grows bigger.*) squelchy gums
(**Cabbie***'s smile grows bigger.*) a certain benefit in the trade i
hear

Cabbie (*nods gleefully*)   i see

Old Woman   so make sure he knows

Cabbie   any other signs are there

Old Woman   what

Cabbie   well if it was cold you couldn't very well bare
your ankles

Man   no no that's true

Old Woman   oh there was one there was one

Cabbie   well what *was* it

Old Woman   hold on a mo (*She thinks then suddenly
remembers.*) pigtails (**Waitress***'s face drops then smiles defiantly.*)

Waitress   time up everyone (**Cabbie** *looks up and stares at*
Waitress *who puts her shoe and sock on the table and pulls out the
small pad from inside her garter strap and the small pencil from behind
her ear.*) now who wants business (**Waitress** *smiles at them all.*)

The storm grows fiercer outside.

Old Woman   i want salt beef and a potato latka

Waitress   salt beef (*She jots it down.*) potato latka

Old Woman   here why is the service so slow

Waitress   well if you must know i was tending to the other waitress (*glares at* **Old Woman**) alright

Cabbie   oh gladi wotsit was it (*He nods comprehendingly.*) i see

Waitress *looks surprised.*

Man   he asked

Waitress (*smiles wryly*)   taken an interest has he (**Cabbie** *frowns noncommittally.*) interesting

Cabbie   why

Waitress   you're just her type

Cabbie (*looks over towards* **Russian**)   are you sure bcos i don't wanna make a fool of myself

Waitress   no no she likes simple men that's who she gets dolled up for

Cabbie   what

Waitress   that's right innit

Cabbie   simple huh

Man   just act dumb son

Cabbie   not too smart you mean

Man   yeh nothing flash

Cabbie   tittle tattle

Man   idle chat

Cabbie (*nods solemnly*)   yeh i think i can manage that

Man   best way to enter a woman's pants

Waitress *and* **Cabbie** *gape at* **Man**.

Cabbie   oh is that so blimey he's piped up a bit this one look at him all of a sudden he's god's gift to blooming women and he's giving me *tips* on the blooming subject can you *believe* that

Man   just having some fun

Cabbie   oh is that *so* mate

Man   i'm having a rare ol time yeh

Waitress   happy we call him

Cabbie   happy

Man   if you want yeh

Cabbie   helping me now are you mate well go on then see what drastic affect you can have on me (**Man** *stares back at* **Cabbie**.) well go on

Man   i never said that

Cabbie   is that the secret then then is it casanova

Man   acting dumb son

Cabbie   that must be where i've erred all these years

Man   with birds

Cabbie   i've been coming over too intellectual

Waitress   probably

Cabbie (*taps his temple*)   i like to dazzle em with a bit of higher stuff

Man   like what

Cabbie   well i dunno

Man   say something

Waitress   politics

Man   religion

Cabbie (*scoffs*)   nah don't be soft

Man   what then

Cabbie   cooking

Waitress *and* **Man** *stare at* **Cabbie** *nonplussed.*

Waitress   yeh that must be the reason

Cabbie   i like to impress a bit you know what i mean show em i read the papers

Waitress   the cookery page

Cabbie   for instance

Man   i used to do that

Cabbie   oh look he's piped up again . . .

Waitress   didn't work

Man   turn up at shindigs all spruced up

Cabbie (*looks taken aback*)   who (**Man** *looks indignant.*) you

Man   i have nice threads

Cabbie   where are they

Man   i like to dress down

Cabbie   why

Waitress   those who have *disguise* the fact allegedly

Cabbie (*looks* **Man** *up and down*)   you must have a lot then

Waitress   it's an english trait

Cabbie (*scoffs*)   oh i know that love it began in india when the hoi polloi conquered the place remember mahatma fucking gandhi and all that

Waitress   so

Cabbie   well they didn't wanna be recognised i mean they weren't exactly fucking *revered* . . .

Waitress   no

Cabbie   so they dressed like pakis

Old Woman   ooh i could *kill* for a cup of tea

Cabbie (*beckons* **Man** *closer*)   here listen to this my boy goes to school

Waitress   does he

Old Woman   well there's an interesting anecdote

Cabbie (*snarls at* **Old Woman**)   well wait a blooming minute

Man   state school

Cabbie (*double takes at* **Man**)   what

Man   like your daughter

Cabbie   same shitty one yeh

Man   shame

Cabbie (*stares back at* **Man**)   shares a class with a fucking paki

Waitress   pakistani sir

Old Woman   what was that dear

Waitress   i think they're called

Cabbie   no this one's from bangladesh

Old Woman   oh

Cabbie   of course he's not the *only* one – no – the place is *rife* – chinks – half breeds – you name it they're fucking there

Man   so why pick on one

Cabbie   bcos he's different this lad

Waitress   how

Cabbie   that's why i mention him you see or that's why my boy mentioned him to me

Man   why

Cabbie   first day he went to school he came back and told me all about him – no messing – no prompting – *nothing* – dya know what i mean

Man   not really no

Waitress   how can you sir he's not saying anything

Cabbie   my little *boy* i'm chatting about

Waitress   yeh we gathered

Cabbie   my little *boy* – comes home from school – something to say – tugs at my shirt – his ol man – *me* – like this (*He tugs at* **Old Woman**'s *shirt.*) look

Old Woman   what

Cabbie   dad dad

Old Woman   what is it son

Cabbie   dad

Old Woman   what's the matter love

Cabbie   dad

Old Woman   is he going mad

Cabbie   dad he says (*He starts blubbing.*) dad (*He wipes away a tear with his napkin.*) my little lad

Waitress *and* **Man** *look at each other quizzically.*

Old Woman   there there lovely (*She strokes* **Cabbie** *affectionately.*)

Cabbie   it's alright missus

Old Woman (*sneers at* **Waitress**)   what has she been saying

Cabbie   my little boy comes home from school

Old Woman   well you do at that age

Cabbie   can't control his pulse poor soul he's that keyed up

Old Woman   oh what made her so

Cabbie   paki in a suit missus

Man   what

Waitress   paki*stani* sir

Cabbie   that's it missus off the estate

Waitress   a suit

Old Woman   are you sure

Cabbie   a cheap one

Waitress   yeh but still . . .

Cabbie   shirt all starched

Man   shiny buttons

Cabbie   shoes gleaming

Man   side parting

Cabbie   cleanly shaved . . .

Waitress   little kid

Cabbie   all the *same* you know what these pakis are like mate they start sprouting at blooming *birth*

Waitress   blimey

Cabbie (*checks*)   my sentiments *exactly* mate (*He nods at* **Man** *concurringly*.) blimey (**Man** *stares back at* **Cabbie** *impassively*) briefcase

Waitress what

Cabbie turns up for school on his first day in a cheap suit and matching fucking briefcase (*He shakes his head incredulously.*) dear oh dear (*He shakes his head incredulously.*) little paki off the estate – poppadom they called him he shares a bed with ten blooming siblings and comes to school like he's bill fucking *gates* (*He points at* **Man**.) now *that* you'd tell your dad about (**Man** *stares back at* **Cabbie** *impassively.*) they all met their new geography teacher so he told me

Man did he

Cabbie concorde they dubbed her

Waitress on account of her nose

Cabbie that's it

Waitress (*looks dumbstruck*) same one *we* had

Cabbie so she introduces herself – hello kids i'm mrs concorde – how dya do and so forth – then they say *their* names – hello miss i'm little poppadom – i'm little onion fucking *bhaji* me – chicken tikka massala – then she runs through geography – now you must remember these kids are from housing estates in deepest fucking deptford for fuck sake i mean they care for geography like my ol mum does for flipping *trance* music – dya know what i mean

Man bless her

Cabbie so – well that's right mate – who gets geography she goes this concorde bitch – all middle fucking class – who can explain it – geography – of course these kids all look at her like she has three fucking *heads* or something this bitch – all except poppadom – his arm is stuck in the air and he's munching at the bit poor cunt i mean he can hardly fucking *contain* himself – yeh poppadom she goes and he explains – inch blooming perfect – well by now you can guess how flaming popular he is i mean not only has he a matching suit from burtons and shiny fucking shoes and a polyester frigging briefcase but he's also a bright spark – and he's a

paki – i mean he's hardly endearing himself to the idiot
fucking *fraternity* is he – anyway that's right she goes
geography is exactly that – well done son – and he sits down
all lovely – so let's have a *harder* question this time she goes
ol big nose – silly bitch – who knows the capital of – now
you must remember these kids don't even know their own
fucking *names* let alone any flaming *capitals* – i mean asking
them a fucking *capital* is like asking a fucking *farm* animal the
price of *toothpaste* – i mean they can hardly fucking wipe
their *arses* this lot – they don't even know the capital of
england – *scotland* they think it is – on my life – they think
scotland is the capital of england – they think *wales* is the
capital of scotland – that's what we're fucking dealing with –
spain is the capital of kuala lumpur – i mean this is *deptford*
darling sunny fucking deptford but no no she thinks she's in
highgate fucking village chatting to a bunch of brain soldiers
so she asks em all the capital of . . . (*He shakes his head
incredulously.*)

Man   what

Cabbie   wait for it

Man   well

Man *and* **Cabbie** *stare at each other.*

Cabbie   bolivia

Man   no

Cabbie (*nods at* **Man** *confirmingly*)   ˙on my life mate

Waitress   bolivia

Cabbie   bo-fucking-livia

Old Woman   what was that honey

Cabbie   bolivia missus

Old Woman   who did

Cabbie   when

Old Woman   what

Cabbie   can you imagine

Old Woman   why

Cabbie   silly sort (*He chuckles to himself deridingly.*) asking a bunch of spotty fucking herberts the capital of bollicking bolivia – i mean i'm a fucking cabbie and *i* don't even know (*He clocks* **Waitress**.) do *you*

Waitress   no

Cabbie   no of course not i mean look at her

Waitress   why should i

Cabbie   why the fuck should you why the fuck *should* she mate – hey – who the fuck flaming *cares* (**Man** *and* **Waitress** *clock each other nonplussed.*) anyway you can picture the poor kids fucking faces – bolivia they're thinking – racking their fucking heads – bolivia – bo-fucking-*livia* – they haven't even heard of *earth* – so there they are toodling their thumbs when guess what . . .

Man *leaps to his feet with his arm stuck in the air and champing at the bit like the eager school kid he once was.*

Man   i know i know

Cabbie (*checks*)   what

Man   ol poppadom (**Cabbie** *and* **Waitress** *gape at* **Man**.) leaps to his feet again (*Sits back down embarrassed.*)

Cabbie   that's right

Man (*shrugs*)   just guessing

Cabbie *and* **Waitress** *look taken aback.*

Cabbie   you know a lot about all of this

Man (*feigns surprise*)   oh am i right then

Cabbie   spot on mate yeh

Man   so he leaps to his feet again then this poppadom then and then what (**Cabbie** *stares back at* **Man** *uncertainly.*) well

Cabbie   goes absolutely 'potty'

Man (*titters to himself*)   i bet he does

Cabbie (*raises his voice*)   miss miss he hollers

Old Woman (*jolts*)   what

Cabbie (*raises his voice further*)   miss

Old Woman   has she been teasing you again

Cabbie   what

Old Woman   will you leave him alone . . .

Waitress   i haven't *done* anything you stupid cow

Old Woman   i've told you he's not *interested* in you none of them is so why don't you just keep your grubby paws to yourself you treacherous little . . .

Man   steady *on* darling

Old Woman   well we was all fine until she came along wiggling her hips . . .

Cabbie   no no that's just the way she *walks* love

Old Woman   all dolled up and *pouting*

Waitress   pouting (*She gapes.*) who (*She scoffs incredulously.*) me

Old Woman   it won't work darling no no not this time we can see right through you and none of us is *interested*

Man   calm down angel i think you musta *misheard* her or something

Waitress   thank you sir honestly i dunno what she's banging *on* about

Cabbie   yeh you'll do yourself a mischief lovely besides i was *talking* remember or don't i exist anymore

Waitress   she's having one of her turns that must be it

Man   oh yeh

Cabbie   what turns are these

Waitress   don't worry i'll soon sort it

Man *gapes at the scene before him but* **Cabbie** *pulls his attention back to him.*

Cabbie   anyway so ol poppadom remember . . .
(**Waitress** *clumsily positions herself so that* **Man** *can't see her pull off* **Old Woman**'s *wig over her eyes.* **Cabbie** *is aware of all this but pretends not to be.*) remember

Waitress   there that's *much* better

Old Woman *sits there speechless. Every so often she discreetly raises her hands to readjust her wig but stops as soon as she thinks she may be noticed.*

Cabbie   *remember*

Man   oh yeh

Cabbie   yeh poppadom she goes . . .

Man   who does

Cabbie   ol big *nose* of course

Man   oh of course yeh

Cabbie   'la paz' he says

Man   er . . . (*He looks at* **Cabbie** *nonplussed.*)

Waitress   la la what

Cabbie   precisely mate

Waitress   la paz

Cabbie   cool as you blooming like

Waitress   is that a place

Cabbie   well what dya blooming think

Waitress   he coulda been bluffing

Cabbie   ol poppadom

Waitress   you never know

Cabbie   no not this boy

Waitress   so how did he know

Cabbie   little pakistani –

Man   ten years old –

Cabbie   ten fucking years –

Man   knows the capital of bolivia –

Cabbie   wears a fucking suit –

Man   shiny fucking shoes

Waitress   shaves in the morning

Cabbie   *shaves* in the morning thank you darling

Waitress   anytime lovely

Cabbie   i couldn't fucking *believe* it – i said no no son there's some mistake – some mistake son there's gotta be – none he said – we was shooting the breeze – me and him – through the night – he couldn't stop *talking* about him – he was awestruck – awestruck he was on my life – my little lad – his mouth was wide open – like this (**Cabbie** *gawps gormlessly with his mouth wide open.*) look (**Cabbie** *again opens his mouth and gawps gormlessly. He clocks* **Man** *out of the corner of his eye.*) dya see

Man   yeh (**Cabbie** *again opens his mouth wide and gawps gormlessly.*) so what happened then to this poppadom

Cabbie   oh he's still there oh yeh (*He nods.*) still in a suit

Man   bullied

Cabbie (*gasps*)   they won't leave him alone

Man   poor sod

Cabbie   it begun that first day and never stopped

Man   yeh but i take it your lad doesn't partake

Cabbie   oh he used to *sure*

Man (*checks*)   what

Waitress   shame on him

Cabbie   he was the blooming *instigator*

Man   are you *sure* about this

Cabbie   he used to call him *all* sorts – well they *all* did – teacher's pet – paki – i mean this kid has had nothing but grief since day one then one day they have a row

Man   who

Cabbie   he and my lad

Man   over what

Cabbie   over nothing – there's a flare up in the canteen – i dunno (*He chuckles to himself.*) can you imagine

Man   what

Cabbie   my boy woulda fucked him up

Man   you mean he didn't

Cabbie   nah nah he couldn't be fucked – just called him a paki – cunt – walked away – now you'd have thought ol poppadom would be pleased – i mean he's just been spared a blooming beating – but no no he trots after my lad and stops him

Man (*looks shocked*)   do what

Cabbie   *dead* (**Man** *gapes at* **Cabbie**) – says what was that matey

Man (*shakes his head to himself in awe*)   i mean the *balls*

Cabbie   now you must remember this kid's been called a paki all his waking life and he's just this minute chosen to be *riled* . . .

Man (*shakes his head to himself in awe*)   dear lord

Cabbie   what was that matey he goes – he calls him matey like they're long lost pals

Man   now that's a nice touch

Cabbie   er – paki i think says my lad now can i go – er – no no you can't says poppadom

Man   oh *does* he now

Cabbie   getting bolder by the minute – i mean he's causing quite a stir – taking the piss somewhat – not good – in front of the whole school – cruising for a blooming bruising if he's careless but no no my lad shows commendable restraint and gives him another go – come again he says – all calm – like his dad – come again – it's always the same says poppadom – er – what is says my lad – – each time you're at a loss it just blurts out – dunnit – what does – paki says poppadom – all fucking hurt – paki – he was making some sorta point

Man (*nods*)   yeh i thought he was

Cabbie   i mean that's fucking funny innit

Waitress   what is

Cabbie   well a paki saying paki

Waitress   i suppose

Cabbie   that just shows how little occurs (*He taps his temple.*) upstairs (*He raises his eyebrows.*) you know what i mean

Man   but you said he was bright

Cabbie (*looks stumped*)   whatever – paki he repeats – paki – you always calls me paki he bleats – well that's bcos you *is* one says my son

Waitress   witty

Cabbie   i have a *name* he goes you can use it if you like you don't always have to call me *paki*

Man   fucking *hell*

Cabbie   precisely

Man   the balls on *him*

Cabbie   like a sparrow in a flipping cage

Man   he *sounds* it mate i can't believe he did that did he really *do* that are you *sure* . . .

Cabbie   screaming his name all *over* the place

Waitress   and what was it

Cabbie   what

Waitress   his real name

Cabbie (*looks stumped*)   well i dunno they called him poppadom

Waitress   what even after all *that*

Cabbie   oh no no nothing *changed*

Man   and what about your lad

Cabbie   well he was the same he couldn't care *less*

Man   no

Cabbie   no no especially *now* of course

Man   why what happened now

Cabbie (*stares back at* **Man** *intently*)   who said something happened

Waitress   something musta (**Cabbie** *stares back at* **Man** *intently*.)

Cabbie   nothing

Waitress   then what

Cabbie   he has other *concerns* put it that way (*He stares back at* **Man** *intently*) okay

Man   i see

Cabbie   he can't be getting all dewy eyed over some silly cunt being *picked* on now can he no not in *his* state

Waitress   what state

Cabbie (*stares back at* **Man** *intently*)   he has his *own* misfortunes to stew on

Waitress   what are they

Cabbie   *bigger* ones (*He stares back at* **Man** *intently*.) that's all

Waitress   bigger ones

Cabbie (*clocks* **Waitress** *tensely*)   i just *said*

Waitress   can you explain

Waitress *and* **Man** *stare intently at* **Cabbie** *who stares back and opens his arms indignantly*.

Cabbie   well can i blooming order or what

The storm grows fiercer outside.

Part Two

Waitress so come on then what shall it be (*She raises her bare foot and shoves it in the groin of* **Man** *who winces in pain. Her garter strap is again revealed. She licks the tip of her pencil and holds out her pad.* **Man** *can finally see* **Old Woman**.) well

Cabbie missus (*He clocks* **Old Woman** *and feigns shock.*) missus

Man what on *earth* . . .

Cabbie *rises and violently pulls old woman's wig above her eyes but ensures it sits crooked instead. He pulls out a comb from his back pocket and begins ruffling her hair even more under the pretence of tidying it.*

here let me help

Waitress no no she's alright she's just attention seeking

Man no no i insist

Waitress *grits her teeth and rubs her foot seductively against* **Man***'s groin.*

Waitress just sit down charlie (*She smiles at* **Man** *who smiles back and strokes her bare thigh seductively.*)

Cabbie there you are missus what happened

Old Woman i could eat something

Cabbie of course you can dear go on give miss lollipop your order

Waitress you poor thing

Cabbie she'll soon fetch it

Waitress of course i shall

Cabbie there you are you see

Old Woman well i want . . .

Waitress *jots it down.*

Cabbie   salt beef

Old Woman   salt beef

Waitress   salt beef mrs cider

Cabbie   that's it

Old Woman   and a potato latka

Waitress   potato latka

Cabbie   smashing

Waitress   and you sir

Cabbie   another lager

Waitress   another lager (*She lifts her bare foot from* **Man**'s *groin then takes off her other shoe and puts it on the table.*)

Cabbie   well i'm glad that's blooming sorted i'm blooming *gasping* over here

Old Woman   i hope she's quicker this time

Waitress   oi have i done something to upset you (*She glares at* **Old Woman**.) i had pressing *matters* before (**Old Woman** *stares back at* **Waitress** *blankly*) she's full of attitude today i dunno why

Cabbie   perhaps it's bcos of *you* mate

Man   what

Cabbie (*indicates* **Old Woman**)   maybe your presence stirs something in her (*He raises his eyebrows suggestively.*) you never know

Man (*tuts dismissively*)   no no that ain't it

Waitress   no no it's to do with *me*

Cabbie   yeh but you're not yourself today love are ya perhaps on *his* account

Waitress *scoffs dismissively.*

no no i'm telling you mate she ain't

Man   well mrs cider

Old Woman   you think you can ensnare a man

Waitress (*checks*)   what

Old Woman   but you can't

Waitress   oh and why not

Old Woman   bcos he's *dead* darling (*They all stare at* **Old Woman** *nonplussed.*) get it

Cabbie   er – who is darling

Old Woman   my doting husband

Cabbie   yeh yeh we *know* he's blooming *dead* blimey he's the lucky one

Old Woman   so put your bits back away and scoot off now *there's* a good girl

Waitress *glares at* **Old Woman**.

Cabbie   well you *heard* her

Waitress   i never even *knew* her cunting husband

Man   no

Waitress   miserable *sod*

Cabbie   miserable was he missus

Old Woman   what

Cabbie   your hubby

Old Woman   no no he was most *entertained*

Waitress   yeh but by *whom* (**Man** *and* **Cabbie** *both draw their breath sharply.*) hey (**Old Woman** *gapes at* **Waitress**.) who kept his pecker up in the long hours

Old Woman   well how *dare* you . . .

Man   now now come on love she hasn't really done anything

Cabbie *scoffs wryly.*

Waitress   why *thank* you sir

Old Woman   she doesn't *have* to does she it's written all *over* her

Man   what is dear

Old Woman   what was your daughter again

Man   a harlot

Old Woman   yeh that's it

Cabbie   oi hold up a minute . . .

Old Woman   she's a silly ol *slag* . . .

Cabbie   my *daughter* . . .

Waitress   hear *hear* missus

Cabbie   oi hold up a *second* . . .

Old Woman   just like *this* one here (*She indicates* **Waitress.**)

Waitress   oh are we jealous mrs cider

Old Woman   what

Waitress   well i mean i can't help it if men covet me

Cabbie   which men darling

Old Woman   where

Waitress   i mean just bcos you're old and grey

Man   hey

Old Woman   i maybe so love but i still have my wits about me

Cabbie (*scoffs*)   oh fuck off do you love you can't even *walk* . . .

Man   oi steady *on* mate . . .

Cabbie   you're a decrepit old *spastic* darling (**Old Woman** *stares back at* **Cabbie** *helplessly*.) face facts

Old Woman   what keeps *keeping* her this one

Cabbie   i dunno love she reckons she had pressing *matters* before

Old Woman   and what were *they* i wonder

Cabbie (*clocks* **Waitress** *who glares at him*)   gladi wotsit you said

Waitress   and what about it

Man   oh did you sort it all out

Cabbie   oh yeah sort *what* out

Man   they had things to discuss

Waitress   oi do you *mind* . . .

Cabbie   no not really

Waitress   that's private

Cabbie   what is

Man   she impedes on her section

Waitress   er . . .

Man   you see this is hers and that one there's *hers* but sometimes she wanders into this

Cabbie   oh *does* she now

Waitress   russian bitch

Man *and* **Cabbie** *look taken aback.*

Cabbie   ohh so she treads on your toes does she

Waitress *glares at* **Cabbie**.

Man   kinda yeh

Cabbie (*nods knowingly*)   oh *i* get it

Waitress   what

Cabbie   touch of rivalry there

Waitress *smirks dismissively*.

i mean just bcos she has a large chest . . .

Waitress (*scoffs*)   it may be large but it sure needs structural work

Cabbie   and skinny legs

Waitress   what

Cabbie   that's no reason to *despise* her darling

Waitress (*glares at* **Cabbie**)   it has nothing to do with that

Cabbie   no no of course not love

Waitress   she's all cosmetic anyway (*She sneers at* **Russian** *off stage.*)

Cabbie   yeh yeh of course

Waitress   but beneath the surface . . .

Cabbie   yeh

Waitress   there lies . . .

Cabbie   what

Waitress   a desperate woman

Cabbie*'s face drops*.

Cabbie   well bloody get her *over* here . . .

Waitress   oi fuck *off* . . .

Cabbie (*checks*)   oh i see (*He nods at* **Waitress** *knowingly.*) territorial is it

Waitress   what

Cabbie   bit possessive are ya love (**Waitress** *glares back at* **Cabbie**.) something dear to your heart got whisked away

Man   you're not wrong *there* mate

Waitress   oi *shut* it you (*She glares at* **Man** *who feigns innocence.*)

Man   what

Cabbie (*nods comprehendingly*)   oh yeh it's all falling into *place*

Old Woman   what is darling

Cabbie   got her comeuppance did she

Old Woman   it *seems* that way

Cabbie   russia musta stole the heart of one of lollipop's luscious *loverboys* . . .

Old Woman   fancy

Man   no no you got it all wrong

Waitress (*nods vindicatedly*)   you *see*

Man   russia didn't steal anyone

Waitress   why *thank* you sir

Man   it was bratislava

Waitress (*checks*)   what

Cabbie   no no sorry mate brata-*who*

Waitress   oi fuck off i told you it was all fucking *over* . . .

Cabbie   *what* was

Waitress   i wasn't *seeing* him anymore

Cabbie   *who*

Man   oh she was seeing a greasy chipmonk mate

Old Woman   lollipop

Cabbie   that's *right* missus

Man (*shakes his head adamantly*)   no no russia's blameless in all of this

Waitress (*glares at* **Man**)   why are you defending her now

Man   who says

Waitress   before you hadn't a good word for her when you first came in

Man   er – no no that was you love

Waitress   oh so she knows her job better than me now is *that* what you mean

Cabbie   no no not at *all* love

Old Woman   well it wouldn't be *hard*

Man   i'm merely stating that you and her wouldn't attract the same *men* (**Cabbie** *scoffs.*) that's all

Cabbie   yeh you can say that again

Man   so she couldn't steal your man even if she tried

Waitress (*looks flattered*)   no no of course not sir thank you

Cabbie   bratislava however had *no* fucking trouble it seems

Waitress   yeh well she soon regretted that sir (*She smiles wryly to herself.*)

Man   oh

Cabbie   how come

Man   he left her then

Cabbie   who did

Waitress   yeh *kinda* sir

Man   antonio

Cabbie (*raises his eyebrows*)   oh really

Man   the previous chef she says he was a bit of a stud

Cabbie   antonio

Man   and that's why she left here

Waitress   well i dunno she just disappeared one day

Old Woman   that's *right* she did very strange I thought

Man   oh so you *knew* her then did you darling

Waitress   and we just *assumed* it was bcos of him

Cabbie   well of course it was i mean why *else* would she blooming leave

Old Woman   i dunno but she had it made here what with all the tips and so forth

Waitress   yeh and me doing all the bloody *work*

Old Woman   yeh you're a flaming *workaholic* love

Waitress   and my antonio in the kitchen of course giving her a service every chance he got i mean she couldn't believe her bloody *luck* . . .

Man   no no i'm *sure*

Waitress   especially as she shouldn't have been here sir

Man   what

Waitress   well you know . . . (*She checks.*)

Man   no

Waitress   she was an imposter sir

Man   what dya mean

Waitress   parading like that and her not even from here (*She tuts disdainfully.*)

Man   you turned her in

Cabbie   what

Old Woman (*gapes at* **Waitress**)   no

Waitress   who said

Cabbie   had her sent home did you love back to brata bleeding blah blah

Man   surely *not*

Man *and* **Cabbie** *gape at* **Waitress** *who smirks dismissively.*

Cabbie   blimey you *are* a dark horse

Waitress   no no hold up . . .

Cabbie   hark at *her* lovely

Man   you cost her her job and the bloke she loved and all bcos they *wanted* each other (*He shakes his head dumbfoundedly.*)

Old Woman   no

Waitress (*smirks dismissively*)   come off it

Cabbie   no no well *done* love (*He nods at* **Waitress** *approvingly.*) and there you was being all sniffy towards me

Waitress   what

Cabbie   turning your nose up at me oh yeh i saw ya

Old Woman (*nods concurringly*)   that's right she did

Cabbie   and all the while you was nothing but a snitch (*He shakes his head dumbfoundedly.*) blimey

Waitress   well she was taking an english girl's job

Cabbie (*nods ironically*)   of course she was darling

Man   what like *her* you mean (*He indicates* **Russian** *off stage.*)

Waitress   what (*She turns to see* **Russian** *off stage then clocks* **Man** *who gapes at her.*) no

Man   she comes here she takes the trouble to take the train and come all the way here

Waitress   no no she came by plane sir

Man   revisit an old stamping ground

Waitress   no no she'd never been here before sir that was her first time

Old Woman (*scoffs*)   yeh and her *last* one as well

Man   go back to stand outside the gates of a place where . . . (*checks*)

Cabbie   where what mate

Man   look at . . . (*checks*)

Cabbie   what mate

Man   kosher harrys should be a *haven* it always *was* a fucking haven what's going *on* here

Waitress   a haven from *what*

Cabbie   what are you *chatting* about

Waitress (*smirks*)   i dunno he's lost *me* mate

Man   salt beef and chips a few quid a bit less for kids

Cabbie   what kids

Old Woman   where

Cabbie   hey

Waitress   there's no kids in *here* love

Man   and they always looked after you – nursed your bruises – gave you some soup

Old Woman   who did

Waitress   what

Man   this is where you escape you run round the corner to flee the fuckers from . . . (*checks*)

Waitress   what

Man   and for what

Cabbie   hey

Man   you come in on a morning with nothing but hope – nothing but good intentions – nothing but a desire not to be noticed and someone decides there's something *wrong* with you do they

Waitress   no no i never laid a finger on her and i'm *proud* of that

Man   how hard was it for her to get up and get dressed and make her way here on a morning

Waitress   she only lived round the *corner*

Man   how the fuck *could* you darling

Waitress (*raises her voice*)   well she *deserved* it

Man (*raises his voice*)   but she hadn't done anything *wrong*

Waitress (*raises her voice further*)   i told you you're a *man* you don't understand

Man (*raises his voice further*)   yeh but you and him was *over* darling

Cabbie   oh *was* they now

Waitress (*raises her voice further*)   no no you're missing the *point* sir

Cabbie   even so that's a bit bloody low love even by *my* blooming standards (*chortles to himself*) dya know what i mean (*shakes his head to himself dumbfoundedly*) blimey

Waitress   so what was it we wanted (*composes herself and licks the tip of her pencil and holds out her pad*) let me see . . . (*looks up at the others who stare back at her dumbfoundedly*) sir (*stares back at* **Man**) sir

Man (*shakes his head dumbfoundedly*)   i sensed a vicious streak in ya love but never that *bad*

Cabbie   no no i agree mate it's shocking

Old Woman (*nods concurringly*)   shocking it is

Cabbie   awful

Old Woman   *awful*

Cabbie   out of order

Old Woman   bang out of order

Cabbie   yeh yeh alright love

Waitress   well i dunno what you're complaining *for* i mean if it wasn't for me and what i done *she* wouldn't be here and you'd have nothing to *leer* at all day

Cabbie (*gawps at* **Russian** *off stage and frowns to himself*)   no no that's a point

Waitress   you *see* sir

Cabbie   still i'd prefer it if she wasn't barred from this section

Waitress (*smiles at* **Cabbie** *smugly*)   she always was (**Cabbie** *who nods comprehendingly.*) there's rules even *she* must adhere to

Man   and yet she strays

Waitress   you mean she *used* to sir (*She smiles smugly at* **Man** *who nods back approvingly.*) i sorted that little issue out no problem

Cabbie   you mean she won't be stepping this way (*A disheartened* **Cabbie** *leers at* **Russian** *off stage and shakes his head ruefully.*) shame

Man   no no you'll have to go to *her*

Cabbie (*loosens his collar at the prospect*)   blimey

Man   well of course you shall she's russian

Cabbie (*checks*)   so

Man   well they do things another way

Cabbie   what way

Old Woman   the *old* way

Man   a bloke has to make the first move

Waitress   dash in there

Man   get in there

Waitress   get stuck in

Man   stick it *in* her

Waitress *gapes at* **Man**.

Cabbie   are you *sure*

Man   it's the only *way* mate (*He opens his arms and smiles at* **Cabbie**.) trust me

Cabbie *stares back uncertainly and loosens his collar even more.*

Cabbie   i'm a tad out of practice that's all

Waitress   no no that's how antonio seduced me

Cabbie   oh really

Man   exactly

Cabbie   hint of a tint was he

Waitress   spanish

Cabbie (*sneers*)   it's disgusting

Waitress   he did all the running

Cabbie   i don't wanna *know* darling alright

Waitress   well you asked

Cabbie   paki bastard

Waitress   it was a curse honestly

Man   why

Waitress   well women *loved* him

Man   but he was faithful

Waitress   what

Man   while he was with you

Waitress   well of *course* he was

Cabbie   yeh *sort* of missus

Old Woman   what was that

Cabbie   well he was *spanish* mrs cider

Old Woman   oh i see (*She nods comprehendingly.*) never mind dear

Man   no no never mind

Cabbie   no moral fucking fibre the spanish (*He frowns disapprovingly.*) none at all (*He sneers disdainfully.*) disgusting (*He ogles* **Russian** *off stage.*) what was the russian's name

Old Woman   gladiola

Cabbie   that's it (*He nods admiringly.*) and you reckon she might be partial

Man   definitely

Cabbie *looks over towards* **Russian** *and struts his head cockily.*

Cabbie   yeh i might chance me arm there

Man   just remember to be forceful

Cabbie   what

Waitress   like antonio

Cabbie (*scoffs*)   yeh but he had it *easy* didn't he i mean she hardly seems discerning this one i mean *look* at her

Old Woman   she's absolutely *gagging* for it

Cabbie   that's *right* missus

Old Woman   some of us ladies keep certain *standards*

Cabbie (*scoffs*)   well whatever they *are* love they weren't enough to keep your *husband* in line

Old Woman   what

Cabbie (*looks confused*)   were they love

Old Woman (*gapes at* **Cabbie**)   who told you

Cabbie   er – told me what

Old Woman   what

Man (*indicates* **Waitress**)   well *she* did a minute ago remember she cast aspersions on your husband's nocturnal liaisons

Old Woman   oh

Cabbie (*twigs*)   you mean she was right

Waitress   there you see i *told* you

Old Woman   no

Cabbie   fuck a *duck heck* missus

Old Woman   what

Cabbie   your husband (*They all gape at a helpless* **Old Woman**.) played the field (*They all gape at a helpless* **Old Woman**.) blimey

Old Woman   it wasn't his fault

Waitress (*scoffs*)   oh no

Man   whose was it

Old Woman   *hers*

Man   whose

Old Woman   the *waitress*

They all gape at **Old Woman** *then turn to face* **Waitress**.

Waitress   well don't look at *me* i never even *knew* her cunting husband

Old Woman   she poisoned him you know

Cabbie   oh took his *life* did she love i hope you told the police

Old Woman   no no she poisoned his *mind* . . .

Cabbie   ohh

Old Woman   tricked him into it i mean he wasn't thinking straight

Waitress   when he married you

Old Woman   she destroyed him (*They all stare at a venomous* **Old Woman** *who glares at* **Waitress**.) ripped out his soul (*She shakes her head to herself mournfully.*) he never recovered

Cabbie   no no i can imagine if he had to return to you after splish-sploshing about with a fit young *bird* i mean what a comedown *that* musta been (*He roars with laughter.*) blimey

Old Woman   she wanted his money but never got it

Man   oh no

Old Woman   i ensured that

Cabbie   oh yeh i bet you did darling i bet you got *every* last penny

Waitress (*smirks dismissively*)   she didn't want his stupid *cash* you silly old *bat* she wanted some *fun* that's all that's all anyone wants these days some flipping *fun* to pass the time i mean let's face facts darling she probably clapped eyes on your dearly departed . . . and liked his looks (**Old Woman** *shakes her head adamantly*)

Old Woman (*smirks dismissively*)   yeh right

Old Woman   sorry

Man   what

Old Woman   he was an ugly sod

Cabbie   well he coulda been well turned out their first meet

Waitress   that's it

Cabbie   nice and neat

Waitress   exactly

Cabbie (*indicates* **Man**)   not like him

Waitress   no

Cabbie   but like me

Waitress   precisely

Cabbie   entirely understandable darling

Waitress (*walks over behind* **Cabbie**)   he made a move on her maybe

Waitress *leans over* **Cabbie** *and starts unbuttoning his shirt and stroking his neck and torso ever so tenderly. All the while she stares intently at* **Man** *who stares back.*

Cabbie   what

Waitress   in her fantasy

Cabbie (*smiles gleefully*)   well come on baby let's pretend

Old Woman   er – what's going on

Man   they're getting acquainted angel

Old Woman (*looks shocked*)   are they getting married

Cabbie   i have to warn you darling i'm taken

Waitress (*whispers seductively in* **Cabbie**'s *ear*)   he whispered sweet nothings in her ear

Cabbie (*giggles childishly*)   oh go on get off

Waitress   i wanna fuck you

Cabbie *looks shocked.*

Waitress   i want your lust

Cabbie   well you're in luck love i'm stocked up today

Waitress   i wanna take you home and strip you off and tie you to the frigging bed posts

Old Woman *gasps in astonishment as* **Waitress** *suddenly throws* **Cabbie** *off his chair and pushes him over the table and violently rips the seat of his trousers and starts simulating fucking him ever so forcefully from behind. Almost as if she were raping him. All the while she stares intently at* **Man** *who stares back.*

Cabbie (*suddenly jolts up and turns to face* **Waitress**)   alright let's go

Waitress   where

Cabbie   back to your place (**Waitress** *gapes at* **Cabbie** *then slaps him hard on the cheek.*) what

Waitress   are you *mad* i wouldn't *touch* you

Cabbie   so what was all *that*

Old Woman   is the wedding off . . .

Waitress   i was merely doing the *do* darling alright

Old Woman   well thank *fuck*

Cabbie   for who

Waitress (*turns slowly to face* **Man**)   someone else present

Man   oh yeh (*stares back at* **Waitress** *impassively.*) who's that then

Waitress (*smiles at* **Man** *seductively while playing with her pigtail*)   now would you care to order

The storm grows fiercer outside.

Man   well at last

Waitress   well go *on* then

Man   a salt beef sandwich

Cabbie   please

Waitress   lean

Cabbie   are you *mad*

Waitress   what

Cabbie   he likes the fat

Waitress   oh is that so

Man   well i must confess

Waitress   oh no no don't be ashamed we all like some flesh on our bonnet (*She puts her foot on* **Cabbie***'s knee and with it pushes him back down on his chair so that her bare thigh is again raised to reveal her garter strap which* **Man** *and* **Cabbie** *gawp at. She leans her pad on her raised knee and licks the tip of her pencil.*) mustard (**Man** *is transfixed.*) charlie

Man (*awakens*)   er – what what

Waitress   mustard

Cabbie   of course

Waitress *jots it down.*

Man   and fries

Waitress   chips

Man   that's it

Waitress   and pickle

Cabbie   a little

Man   what pickle

Waitress   pickle on your *sandwich* lovely

Man   what sorta pickle

Waitress   well i dunno

Man no

Cabbie no

Man oh no i don't think so

Cabbie oh go on have some pickle please be a pickle person peter

Waitress charlie

Cabbie what's your name

Man (*stares back at* **Cabbie** *and* **Waitress**) happy

Waitress *smiles back at* **Man**. **Cabbie** *looks put out by this.*

Cabbie happy (*He looks bemused*.)

Waitress to drink 'happy'

Man water

Cabbie water

Waitress sparkling

Cabbie blimey she's good this one

Man still

Cabbie still what

Man what dya mean

Waitress still

Old Woman what was that

Cabbie i dunno missus i'm losing the blooming thread

Waitress a bottle

Man a bottle

Cabbie (*looks taken aback*) blimey bottled water hark at mister sophisticado

Old Woman what was that

Cabbie (*checks and sneers at* **Old Woman**)   oh give us a break missus they know you can blooming hear

Waitress   and what about *you* mrs cider will you have a drink

Old Woman   oh go on then if it's warm

Cabbie (*his face drops*)   well of *course* it's warm you're not in blooming europe *here* (*He scoffs.*) blimey (*He clocks* **Man**.) she thinks she's in europe bless (**Man** *and* **Waitress** *stare at* **Cabbie** *nonplussed.*) with wotsisname i bet (**Cabbie** *clocks* **Waitress**.) *your* one (**Waitress** *stares back cluelessly.*) the paki

Old Woman   antonio

Cabbie   the paki

Waitress   spanish

Cabbie   blooming spain

Waitress   what about it

Cabbie   well have you ever *been* mate

Man   what

Cabbie (*scoffs dismissively*)   no no of course you wouldn't

Man   no no of course

Old Woman   me and my husband went

Man   oh *did* you darling

Cabbie (*scoffs*)   blimey

Old Woman   we went to this bar

Cabbie   oh *that's* interesting fucking hell

Old Woman   the waitress appears

Cabbie   even *more* blooming riveting

Old Woman   she looked not unlike yourself love (**Waitress** *feigns modesty.*) only she had long black hair and olive skin and pretty eyes and lovely legs and an ample bust and an arse that jutted out like a *baboon's* but apart from that you was almost *twins*

Waitress (*glares at* **Old Woman** *then smiles smugly*)   but could she wait tables

They all gape incredulously at **Waitress** *who smiles smugly at them.*

Man   brian

Cabbie   her husband mate

Old Woman   it came back cold

Man   no

Waitress   aah you see

Old Woman   clumps of ice and everything

Man (*looks shocked*)   what

Old Woman   clumps of ice

Man   in the tea

Old Woman (*nods confirmingly*)   in the blasted tea

Cabbie   what was she a fucking comedian

Old Woman   well that's what *i* said (*She gapes at* **Man**.) she just stared

Man   stared

Old Woman   like i was mad yeh

Man   you

Old Woman   loopy fucking loo

Cabbie   well they're all prejudiced mrs cider

Waitress   well we show ourselves *up*

Cabbie   er . . . (*He checks.*) do what love

Waitress   when we go there

Cabbie   where

Waitress   well we all want egg and chips

Cabbie   who does

Waitress   black pudding

Cabbie   so what

Waitress   well we don't embrace their culture fully that's what riles em

Cabbie (*looks taken aback*)   an expert are you love

Waitress   so antonio reckoned

Cabbie   i mean she scrimps and *saves* all blooming year . . .

Old Woman   no no

Cabbie   to go away

Old Woman   who did

Cabbie   what

Old Woman   *brian* paid for it

Cabbie   and what does she fucking get for it (**Waitress** *stares back at* **Cabbie**.) hey

Man   cold tea

Cabbie   exactly mate (*He clocks* **Man**.) good point

Old Woman   what was that

Cabbie (*sighs wearily*)   cold blooming *tea*

Old Woman   well what about it

Cabbie   what

Old Woman   the tea

Man   well it was *cold* wasn't it

Old Woman *looks nonplussed then takes off her cardigan to reveal a blouse underneath and hands it to* **Man** *who puts it on over his shirt some time later.*

Cabbie   i mean have they not got kettles

Man   what (*He looks stumped.*)

Cabbie   have they not *heard* of the frigging kettle – we go there – spend our money – then what – cold tea like we was cunts – and when you complain they treat you like a frigging *circus* act – frigging freak show on fucking *legs* – warm tea they go – they tell all their friends – mama they scream – papa crazy english papa – crazy english come to kill me – english fucking elephant

Man   bobby charlton

Cabbie (*checks*)   what

Man (*titters to himself*)   bobby fucking charlton they called me over there i mean i look nothing *like* bobby charlton . . . (*They all stare nonplussed at* **Man** *who opens his arms.*) do i

Old Woman   oi i thought you never went

Man   what

Waitress   yeh so did i

Man   who says

Cabbie   what's your blooming game you're up to something

Man   well i went once

Cabbie (*scoffs*)   once or a billion blooming times you still blooming went

Man (*smirks*)   so i went so what

Cabbie (*frowns*)   nothing

Man   i went to spain does that make me a genius

Cabbie (*shakes his head*)   just a cheat

Man   what

Cabbie   cheating people you don't even know i mean what's *wrong* with you

Man   i never cheated anyone or wronged anyone in my life maybe that's where i've been going wrong maybe i need to change that

Cabbie   looks like you already did mate

Man   but it was a passing visit i forgot

Waitress   did something happen in spain sir

Man   what

Waitress   something *bad* maybe

Man (*scoffs dismissively*)   no

Cabbie (*smiles wryly*)   i think you *hit* on something love

Waitress   something dark from your past (**Man** *scoffs dismissively*.) here at home

Cabbie   got bullied at school

Waitress   i can make it better if you want sir make you forget all your woes

Cabbie   take it out on others do you now mate (**Man** *stares back at* **Cabbie**.) play these little games to appease your past

Man (*scoffs*)   what games

Cabbie   i know he doesn't give much *away* this one but what he does you can't even *trust*

Man   i think you're maybe jumping the gun a bit mate

Cabbie   oh are we right then (*He stares back at* **Man** *who opens his arms.*)

Man   tell me why would anyone pick on me

Cabbie (*frowns*)   your dress sense perhaps

Man   you have to be *different* to be bullied

Cabbie   well that could be *it* mate

Waitress   you was singled out bcos of your *singularity* sir

Man (*chuckles to himself*)   but i never was

Cabbie   you *musta* been i mean look at you you scruffy cunt if i'd have gone to school like that . . . (*He sneers at* **Man** *and shakes his head.*)

Man   it wasn't my clothes . . . (*He checks.*)

Cabbie   *games* then

Waitress   oh not too physical are you sir well we can soon change that

Cabbie   not the sporty type was you mate i tell you what it doesn't surprise me

Waitress   if you're willing and open enough

Cabbie   not even *mind* games mate (**Man** *stares back at* **Cabbie**.) more in the brain was ya (**Man** *stares back at* **Cabbie**.) a thinker (*He scoffs derisively.*)

Man   no no you misunderstand

Cabbie   teased a tad was ya

Man   i always fitted in

Waitress   yeh so you said you said you had a *fine* time at school remember

Man   and so i did

Cabbie   humiliated was ya

Man   one of the *boys* i was

Cabbie   you're just like poppadom (**Man** *stares back at* **Cabbie**.) remember him

Man (*mutters to himself*)   how could i forget

Old Woman   sorry what was that

Man   i said i wish i *had* been darling

Cabbie   i mean not as bright clearly

Man   what

Waitress   oh leave him alone

Old Woman   yeh yeh we know you're *keen* on him love

Waitress   well he's different to our regular punters . . .

Old Woman   singular

Waitress   that's it

Cabbie (*feigns being impressed*)   well hark at the *lady* killer in our midst missus i wonder what his *secret* is

Waitress (*scoffs*)   well it's clearly eluded *you*

Cabbie (*clocks* **Waitress**)   what was that

Waitress   a minute ago you was hammering him now you want him to impart all his worldly wisdom

Man   well he needs the tips doesn't he darling

Cabbie   oi what was that

Man   well you're gonna practise a few on ol gladi wola over there in a second (**Cabbie** *glares at* **Man** *who indicates* **Russian** *off stage who* **Cabbie** *then leers at.*) remember

Cabbie   oh yeh

Man   you see you forgot about her you was worrying about me and all the time you was taking your eye off the *ball* mate

Cabbie   so i was yeh yeh thanks mate

Man   you *see*

Cabbie   so what do I do (*He clocks* **Man** *and nods towards* **Russian**.)

Man   pretend you're not fussed

Cabbie   about what

Man   well sex of course

Waitress (*eyes light up*)   why that's *right* sir

Cabbie   are you *sure* about that

Waitress   of course *i'm* not fooled by your nonchalance sir

Old Woman   fussed about what was that did he say

Cabbie   oh give it a *rest* missus

Man   no no she never *heard* . . .

Cabbie (*yells impatiently*)   oh for fuck sake he said *sex*

Old Woman (*gapes at* **Cabbie**)   did he i didn't see it

Cabbie   no no not right *here* . . .

Old Woman   he musta been awful quick an in and out job was it oh yeh my husband was like that

They all stare at **Old Woman** *who nods knowingly.*

Cabbie   well he was probably in a bit of a rush to see wotsername . . .

Waitress   his bit on the side

Cabbie   busty bertha

Waitress   that's it

Man   not a good lover was he mrs cider then your brian

Old Woman   well he was until . . . (*She checks.*)

Man   what

Old Woman   he met . . . (*She sneers.*) i coulda strangled her

Cabbie (*scoffs*)   yeh if you had the strength

Old Woman   hospitalised her

Cabbie (*scoffs*)   are you *sure* about that

Old Woman   confined her to a . . . (*She checks and looks despondently at her wheelchair.*)

Cabbie   i tell you what you coulda *shared* one with her for a hoot

Old Woman   i wouldn't have to i coulda just . . . (*She checks.*)

Man   what

Cabbie   *given* it to her (*He scoffs.*) got up on both feet and said there you go darling it's all yours (*He roars with laughter.*) i know you pretend you're deaf but you ain't *that* cute (*He shakes his head dumbfoundedly.*) blimey (*He roars with laughter.*) i've been wheeling you in my cab for *how* many years (**Old Woman** *stares back at him helplessly.*) wheeling you in here (**Old Woman** *stares back at him helplessly.*) for no fucking fee (**Old Woman** *stares back at him helplessly.*) don't tell me you can *walk* now missus

Waitress (*tuts dismissively*)   of course she can't

Cabbie   no no i know she's just wishful thinking bless her

Waitress   when did you have the accident

Cabbie   oh not *that* again love bloody hell

Old Woman   what accident

Waitress   what

Cabbie   there musta been an accident

Man   she *told* you it coulda been shock

Cabbie   well was it missus

Waitress   the shock of . . .

Cabbie (*nods comprehendingly*)   ohh i *get* it

Waitress   your brian strayed and you lost the power to walk did you darling

They all stare at a helpless **Old Woman**.

Old Woman   no

Waitress   you was knocked for six and instead of standing up you buckled and lost the power of your legs (*They all stare at a helpless* **Old Woman**.) withered away (*They all stare at a helpless* **Old Woman**.) can't even hear can you dear (*She raises her voice.*) i said . . .

Man   she *knows* what you said angel

Cabbie (*raises his eyebrows*)   oh she can hear now can she mate

Man   well i know her better now

Old Woman   that's right we do don't we love (*She smiles fondly at* **Man** *and places her hand on him.* **Cabbie** *looks put out by this.*)

Cabbie   er . . .

Man   Yeh

Cabbie   so it definitely works then this pretending you're not fussed lark (**Man** *stares back at* **Cabbie** *blankly.*) with the *ladies*

Man (*twigs*)   oh yeh

Cabbie   well *fancy* missus

Man   well the idea is you bluff a bird into thinking you're *deep* mrs cider . . .

Cabbie   yeh but not so deep you wouldn't have a mindless *shag*

Man   no no you want her to think you're not *interested*

Cabbie   in bedding her

Man   exactly

Cabbie   what for

Man   so she lets you *bed* her

Cabbie (*stares back at* **Man** *nonplussed*)   of course

Man   comprende amigo

Cabbie   good thinking compadre

Man   hence my adopted guise

Cabbie *and* **Waitress** *stare at* **Man** *who opens his arms.*

Waitress   the scruffy jack look

Man   precisely petra

Waitress   under sell yourself

Man   over compensate later

Cabbie   well whatever it is it sure seems to *work* mate full credit to ya (**Man** *stares back at him impassively.*) and i thought you was a charlatan

Man   no no that's okay

Cabbie   no no i take it all *back*

Man   no no there's no need

Cabbie   no no good going mate i mean she's absolutely *smitten* this one (**Man** *and* **Cabbie** *stare at* **Waitress** *who smiles at* **Man** *seductively.*) look at her

Waitress   and what shall he do about it

Old Woman   nothing

Waitress (*her face drops*)   what

Old Woman   he's just stringing you along aren't you son proving a point to everyone oh yeh i know your game (*She scoffs dismissively.*) no no he has no lust for you love i mean a man like *that* (*She smirks dismissively.*)

Waitress (*glares at* **Old Woman** *then turns and smiles at* **Man**)   well handsome

Old Woman   i bet he's already spoken for or if not there's one in the pipeline i bet he's meeting her here i bet she comes through that door any *minute*

Cabbie   yeh i bet she's a right screamy sort (*He nods knowingly.*) blonde (*He smiles wryly at* **Man**.) blue eyes (*He smiles wryly at* **Man**.) lily white skin (*He smiles wryly at* **Man** *who stares back impassively.*) an english blooming angel oh yeh i know your type mate

Waitress   no no there is no-one he's just toying with you (*They all stare at* **Man**.) aren't you sir (*She tenses.*) well *tell* them (*She smirks.*) he's not right

Man   about one thing maybe

Waitress   and what's that

Man   there *is* someone

Waitress (*her face drops*)   what

Cabbie   *there* you are darling

Man   not exactly as he *described* mind

Cabbie   oh come on mate she has to be a *blonde* (**Man** *stares back at* **Cabbie** *impassively.*) no (**Cabbie** *looks perplexed.*) what then (*He smiles at* **Man** *wryly.*) not telling (*He nods at* **Man** *approvingly.*) like it

Cabbie   that's rich darling coming from *you* i mean you're hardly up front *yourself* . . .

Old Woman   yeh bratislava could vouch for that

Cabbie   well she *could* if she had a clue how she got done

Old Woman   well that's *right* son

Cabbie   no no top *marks* mate (*He nods at* **Man** *approvingly.*) you strung her along something *rotten*

Old Woman   you musta had an *awful* time at school to become so *vindictive*

Cabbie   mind you she's hardly the *sternest* of tests is she this one no not like that russian over there oh yeh now *she's* another story

Man   you should get in there mate (*He indicates* **Russian** *off stage.*)

Cabbie   what

Man   move in like antonio did with her (*He indicates an irate* **Waitress**.)

Cabbie   yeh yeh but she's bang up for it night and *day* isn't she said so herself – she hasn't all these strange rituals you have to get through

Man   what strange rituals

Cabbie   well you said yourself these russians are all old fashioned

Waitress   yeh that's what antonio said

Cabbie   oh look she's piped up again

Waitress (*shakes her head to herself*)   english girls were far *easier* he said

Old Woman (*smirks wryly*)   well if *you* were all he had to go on

Waitress   i said *what* english ones . . .

Cabbie   what

Waitress   *where*

Cabbie   hey

Waitress   tell me and i'll flaming well sort em *out* . . .

Cabbie   and i bet she would *too* mate

Waitress   it turns out the slapper next door in the newsagents is giving him the big fucking come *on* . . .

Cabbie   *no*

Waitress   the tart across the road in the bank yeh – the scrawny cow who works in the fucking coffee shop on the corner (*She winces.*) horrible fucking coffee have you tried it

Cabbie   no

Waitress   well i wouldn't bother

Cabbie   is she still there

Waitress   yeh yeh i think so

Cabbie   oh i might give that a go

Waitress   all over him like bleeding *wallpaper* (**Man** *and* **Cabbie** *stare at* **Waitress** *nonplussed.*) his spanish looks (**Man** *and* **Cabbie** *stare at* **Waitress** *nonplussed.*) his spanish smile (**Man** *and* **Cabbie** *stare at* **Waitress** *nonplussed.*) his tight spanish arse

Cabbie   lovely

Waitress   he walks in and they go *giddy* (**Man** *and* **Cabbie** *stare at* **Waitress** *nonplussed.*) well no wonder he thought like that i put him straight i said no no antonio no – no antonio – he said what – i said that's not a true portrait of english womanhood – please – he said why – i said bcos they're nothing but fucking *scrubbers* look at em . . .

Cabbie   i wish i *could* mate

Waitress   i said *i'm* not easy antonio whatever you fucking say how *dare* you antonio i said how fucking *dare* you calling me easy like that

Man   when was this

Waitress   straight after sex

Cabbie (*nearly chokes*)   what

Waitress   in the kitchen after work

Cabbie   after work

Waitress   what a first day *that* was for him

Cabbie (*gapes at* **Waitress**)   first blooming day (**Waitress** *nods confirmingly.*) blimey

Waitress (*raises her pad and licks the tip of her pencil*)   so a pot of tea mrs cider

Old Woman (*stares at* **Waitress** *blankly*)   did she say tea

Cabbie   darjeeling missus

The storm grows fiercer outside.

Old Woman   nice and warm

Cabbie   off you trot

Waitress (*glares at* **Cabbie**)   what

Cabbie   on your way lovely (**Waitress** *glares at* **Cabbie** *who smiles condescendingly at her.*) ta ra (**Waitress** *turns and walks off.*) blimey i thought she'd never leave

Old Woman   where has she gone

Man   to fetch your tea darling

Old Woman   bring her back i haven't ordered

Man (*checks*)   what

Old Woman   i want salt beef and a potato *latka*

Cabbie (*sighs wearily*)   right that's it i've had enough of your silly games the pair of ya you can rib each other to death for all i care (*Stands.*)

Old Woman   where is he going oh please don't let him go don't let him *leave* me . . .

Man   it's alright darling calm *down*

Cabbie (*struts his head cockily*)   no no it's time that russian bitch witnessed the fine art of english seduction mate

Old Woman *scoffs derisively at* **Cabbie** *who begins to walk off.*

Man   don't forget my tips

Cabbie (*checks and turns to face* **Man**)   oh yeh your pearls of worldly wisdom what were they again

Man   just act dumb son

Cabbie   that's the one

Man   act like a simple cunt

Cabbie (*checks and stares at* **Man**)   how do i act that

Old Woman   don't worry lover you'll be okay

Cabbie (*double takes at* **Old Woman** *then clocks* **Man**)   so how do i look

Man (*studies* **Cabbie** *whose shirt is half undone and whose seat of his trousers is ripped open.*)   a-one (**Cabbie** *struts his head cockily.*)   fool her and you may strike gold (**Cabbie** *pulls off his taxi badge and puts it on the table then rips off his shirt to reveal an unflattering chest.*)   you're just her type remember

Cabbie   blimey (*He summons up some courage.*) well this is it mate

Man   it sure is

Cabbie (*gulps hard*)   shit (*He summons up the courage and begins to waddle off.*)

Old Woman   has he gone to the loo

Man   no no he's gone after that russian waitress that one *there* look (**Old Woman** *gapes in direction of* **Russian**.) what

Old Woman   have they not got bras (**Man** *titters wryly to himself.*) well she doesn't look terribly bright whoever she is

Man   well he may have a chance then

Old Woman (*looks puzzled*)   excuse me

Man   she can't speak english neither

Old Woman   so what

Man   i reckon he could be quids in

Old Woman   er . . .

Man   yeh madam

Old Woman   i think you misinterpret our friend

Man   yeh i wondered about that i mean you two seem an unlikely pair

Old Woman   his was the first cab i found with wheelchair access he had it all done at his own expense

Man   well i bet he profits now

Old Woman   no no it wasn't for that

Man   was it not no

Old Woman   no no it was for his son

Man (*looks surprised*)   his *son* (**Old Woman** *nods.*) wheelchair bound

Old Woman   oh for some years now

Man   what happened

Old Woman   a debilitating disease

Man   contracted

Old Woman   no no he had it all along but it still came as a shock when it struck

Man   i bet it did

Old Woman   the authorities suggested a special school

Man   well that sounds reasonable

Old Woman   special needs

Man   did he take heed

Old Woman   did he heck (*She smirks dismissively.*) up in arms he caused a right ol commotion

Man   why

Old Woman   pride

Man   pride

Old Woman   no no son of mine has a learning problem missus

Man   and does he

Old Woman   what

Man   have problems learning

Old Woman (*checks*)   he can't even stay *awake*

Man   what

Old Woman   he nods off during lessons it's *awful* – snores and *all* sorts – dribbles down his shirt

Man   they didn't kick him out

Old Woman   well they tried

Man   and

Old Woman   he took em to court

Man   what

Old Woman   or one of them tribunals or something

Man   and the boy

Old Woman   well he liked it there he was chuffed he could stay

Man   he was popular

Old Woman (*nods*)   before

Man   oh not anymore

Old Woman (*shakes her head*)   they turned against him

Man   who

Old Woman   the other kids

Man   what

Old Woman   they just can't *talk* to him

Man   you mean he can't communicate

Old Woman   well i mean it takes an awful lot – you have to *really* be interested – drag things out – be bloody patient i can tell you and even if you *do* take the time (*She shakes her head forlornly.*) well

Man   what

Old Woman   he seldom makes any sense

Man   so he has no friends

Old Woman (*shakes her head ruefully*)   just the one

Man (*looks shocked*)   Just the one

Old Woman   poppadom (**Man** *looks taken aback.*) he's the only one who takes the *time*

Man   what is he lonely or something

Old Woman   no no he's a popular lad

Man (*scoffs*)   yeh but surely he remembers

Old Woman   remembers what

Man   being *bullied*

Old Woman   yeh but they're all older now

Man (*raises his eyebrows*)   oh so age brings forgiveness with it does it darling

Old Woman (*looks stumped*)   well i forgive him for his abruptness (*She indicates* **Cabbie** *off stage.*)

Man   oh yeh so you do

Old Woman   you see

Man   tell me why does he resent poppadom so much then if he's his son's only mate (*They both look bemused.*) i don't understand

Old Woman   perhaps bcos he humiliated his lad

Man   you mean that spat they had

Old Woman (*nods*)   in front of the whole school

Man   he's still upset about *that*

Old Woman   well he's upset about something

Man (*smirks wryly*)   yeh that's for sure love

Old Woman   poor ol thing

Man   i can't believe that poppadom can be so *forgiving* towards his son who called him all those rotten things and still *does* according to him (*He indicates* **Cabbie** *off stage.*)

Old Woman   you could manage it

Man (*shakes his head adamantly and smirks to himself*)   no no believe me love the cunt could fall off his chair and be screaming in pain and I'd leave him there to stew in his own fucking *shit* . . .

Old Woman   he shall die soon

Man (*checks and composes himself*)   what

Old Woman   his lad

Man (*gapes at* **Old Woman**)   oh will he

Old Woman (*nods confirmingly*)   he's not got long

Man   and what about *you* you're not gonna pop your clogs

Old Woman   no not unless i die of hunger (*They titter together.* **Old Woman** *spots* **Waitress** *stomp on holding a tray of beverages.*) aye aye

Waitress   here you are mrs cider (*Slams down a cup and saucer and a pot of tea for* **Old Woman**.) lovely (*Slams down a bottle of water for* **Man** *and a second can of lager for absent* **Cabbie**.)

Man   he's not here

Waitress   i know i saw him hard at work

Man   how's he doing

Waitress   well he's talking

Man   he's not tongue tied then

Waitress (*smirks wryly*)   you wish

Man   and her

Waitress   well she's listening (**Man** *smirks wryly*.) at least she seems to be

Old Woman   is he acting dumb

Waitress   pretty much mrs cider

Old Woman   and is he being a cunt

Waitress (*looks taken aback*)   what

Old Woman   i say is he being a *cunt*

Waitress (*nods*)   definitely

Old Woman (*looks inconsolable*)   oh darn

Man   what

Old Woman   he could be about to *score*

Waitress (*scoffs*)   no no i doubt it even with *that* ol slapper

Old Woman   well he might if his tips were spot on

Old Woman *indicates* **Man** *whom* **Waitress** *clocks.*

Man   i gave him a last minute pep talk

Waitress (*sneers at* **Man**)   well no wonder he's doing so well

Man (*opens his arms*)   well there's no point hoarding all your expertise

Waitress (*looks* **Man** *up and down disdainfully*)   no

Man (*smiles at* **Waitress** *smugly*)   no

Waitress   and haven't you shitloads sir (**Man***'s face drops.*)
i mean what the fuck is he *wearing* lovely (**Waitress** *clocks*
Old Woman *who stares back at her blankly.*) right so let's get
this straight then shall we everyone (*Without any ceremony*
Waitress *releases her note pad from inside her garter strap and
studies it.*) you want salt beef

Man   salt beef

Waitress   and a potato latka

Man   potato latka

Waitress   and you sir

Old Woman   a salt beef sandwich

Waitress   not lean

Old Woman   no

Waitress   mustard

Man   mustard

Old Woman   that's right

Waitress   and chips

Old Woman   that's it

Waitress   and pickle

Old Woman   a little

Waitress   and you won't change your mind this time mrs
cider

Old Woman   no no not this time love

Waitress   fine (*She hitches up her skirt again and snaps her pad
back into her garter strap then walks off taking the empty lager can with
her.*)

Old Woman   well she's very thorough (*She watches **Man**
pour her a cup of tea.*) oh you're most kind

Man (*pours himself a glass of water and raises it*)   your health darling

Old Woman   quite charming

She raises her cup and they clink before both gulping down their drinks thirstily. The storm grows fiercer outside. **Man** *pours them both another.*

Man   so he brings you here each week does he that one (**Man** *indicates* **Cabbie** *off stage.* **Old Woman** *nods.*) keeps you company

Old Woman (*scoffs*)   talks at me (*They titter together.*) no no he likes bringing me he pretends not to of course but it gives him something to do something he can tell the wife without getting in trouble i mean this is his weekend he should be at home or out shopping with her or tending to the kids but i think he likes a bit of solace you know some time to unwind some time to contemplate

Man   philosophise

Old Woman   that's right

Man   well he sure makes use of it

They titter together.

Old Woman   no no he's alright really he's been most kind since my brian died

Man   and what did your brian *do* darling

Old Woman   show business

Man (*looks impressed*)   ohh *was* he

Old Woman   that's why we had those parties i spoke of

Man   the celebrity dos

Old Woman (*nods*)   friend to all the stars he was the most glamorous women of their time and they *all* adored him

Man   but he only had eyes for you darling (*He checks.*) i
mean . . . (*He checks.*) except . . . (*He checks.*) apart from . . .
(*He checks.*) he sounds great mrs cider

Old Woman (*nods reflectively*)   we had some fun

Man   of course you did darling

Old Woman   i was a dancer back then

Man (*looks surprised*)   was ya

Old Woman (*nods*)   i danced in this club he used to
frequent and one night we got talking

Man   a charmer was he darling

Old Woman   dead nice he was yeh (*She nods.*) real jewish
gent

Man   i'm sure he was

Old Woman   he complimented my legs

Man   did he that's saucy

They titter together.

Old Woman   said they were the best legs among all the
girls and there were lots of legs there well there were lots of
girls and they each had a *pair*

Man (*stares at* **Old Woman** *nonplussed*)   but yours were the
best

Old Woman   well that's what *he* said anyway we got
married soon after

Man   did ya

Old Woman   mummy and daddy were pleased as punch
bcos it meant i stopped dancing

Man   you mean they didn't approve

Old Woman   well it wasn't jewish they said

Man   was it not no

Old Woman   well you should *know* i mean does *your* mum dance

Man   no not professionally

Old Woman   well there you *are* you see it's not what jews do

Man   so they was pleased you stopped

Old Woman   pleased i stopped pleased i met a nice jewish lad with good prospects

Man   oh loaded was he

Old Woman   well no no not back then but he soon became

Man   i see

Old Woman   with a lot of help from me of course i mean i backed him all the way i stopped working and i took care of things like a good wife should did all the cooking for when he entertained . . .

Man   you never had kids

Old Woman (*checks then looks forlorn*)   brian didn't want any more

Man   *more*

Old Woman (*nods*)   from his previous wife

Man   you mean he left her for you

Old Woman   well she wasn't jewish so it didn't really matter

Man   what

Old Woman   she was wrong for him

Man   who says

Old Woman   well they weren't the same sort (**Man** *stares at* **Old Woman** *nonplussed.*) they were different (**Man** *stares*

at **Old Woman** *nonplussed.*) people shouldn't mix (**Man** *stares at* **Old Woman** *nonplussed.*) not in my book (*She indicates* **Cabbie** *and* **Waitress** *off stage.*) i mean if you really wanna know i don't think they should even let the likes of *them* in here (**Man** *stares at* **Old Woman** *nonplussed.*) mind you i shouldn't complain i'm having a hell of a time today i suppose

Man   oh are you

Old Woman   of course

Man   why's that then

Old Woman   bcos of *you* you silly thing

Man (*looks startled*)   well i'm flattered mrs cider

Old Woman   i could get up and *dance* even

Man   what

Old Woman   yeh hold on a mo (**Man** *looks on in wonder as* **Old Woman** *pulls off her shoes and pushes herself off the wheelchair and up onto her feet.*) here we go

Man   what the fuck . . .

(**Old Woman** *pulls up her skirt to reveal her legs which are adorned with stockings and suspenders and starts dancing exuberantly around the table and singing to herself.*)   tra la la la la la la . . . (**Man** *gapes at* **Old Woman** *and looks around to see if anyone else is watching.*) want to join

Man   no no i'm not the best mover mrs cider

Old Woman (*dances and sings merrily*)   tra la la . . .

Man   so you *was* kidding us

Old Woman   la la la . . .

Man   blimey

Old Woman   i've not had this much fun since . . . (*She checks and seems to wither a tad.*)

Man   what

Old Woman   since . . . (*She withers further.*) since . . . (*She withers further.*) brian . . . (*She runs out of breath.*) since before he . . .

Man   left

Old Woman (*gasps and faints into the wheelchair.* **Man** *watches on impassively as she eventually comes to and looks around her in a daze.*)   what happened

Man   you got up and did a jig

Old Woman   who (**Man** *points at* **Old Woman**.) oh don't be so soft

Man   no no it's *true*

Old Woman   me (*She looks baffled.*) *danced*

Man   you was full of beans until you remembered . . .

Old Woman   here dya wanna see a picture

Man   what (*A surprised* **Man** *watches* **Old Woman** *rummage through her bag.*)

Old Woman   there's one here somewhere

Man   you mean you carry one of *him* around with ya

Old Woman (*pulls out her keys and her purse and puts them on the table. She sticks her hand back inside her bag and pulls out an old picture*)   there you are (*She hands* **Man** *the picture.*) that's on holiday

Man   oh where was this

Old Woman   i'm surprised you don't recognise it

Man   what

Old Woman (*stares at* **Man** *nonplussed*)   spain

Man (*stares back nonplussed*)   ohh with the cold *tea*

Old Woman   that's right you lying toe rag

Man   and who's that saucy dish on his arm

Old Woman   why that's me

Man (*feigns shock*)   no

Old Woman   of course

Man   blimey you was a *sort*

Old Woman (*chortles loudly*)   behave (*She slaps* **Man** *playfully*.) you crafty thing

Man   crafty (*He scoffs*.) me (**Old Woman** *nods*.) i'm not a patch on *you* darling i mean i don't think i've ever *met* such a trickster (*He gapes at* **Old Woman** *and shakes his head in awe*.)

Old Woman   here i can bring you more next week if you like

Man   no no i won't be here

Old Woman   oh just a passing visit is it

Man   i suppose

Old Woman   and for which reason

Man (*looks around the bar*)   nostalgia

Old Woman (*looks surprised*)   at your age

Man   well i used to come here when i was young

Old Woman   oh *did* you (**Man** *nods*.) funny i don't recognise you

Man   well i was better turned out then i suppose

Old Woman   oh i see

Man   have you been coming long

Old Woman (*nods*)   brian first brought me

Man (*nods comprehendingly*)   oh i see

Old Woman   it was almost a second home each saturday three o'clock on the dot our table always ready

Man   not like today hey

Old Woman   no no standards have slipped somewhat

Man (*nods wryly*)   i bet they have

Old Woman   harry brought us our drinks personally (*She stares back smugly at* **Man**.)

Man   harry

Old Woman   the owner

Man (*feigns being impressed*)   well he musta liked you

Old Woman   no not particularly

Man   oh

Old Woman   he liked brian you see everyone liked brian that's why i had so much fun

Man   and what about you

Old Woman   what

Man   did anyone like *you*

Old Woman (*looks at* **Man** *like that was the most stupid question in the world*)   brian did (*She checks.*) well he did until . . . (*She checks.*) she . . . (*She tenses.*)

Man   now now come on love you should vent your spleen elsewhere it might be better for you

Old Woman   on who

Man (*scoffs wryly*)   well i could think of a few

Old Woman   oh yeh

Man   well that waitress for one i mean what the fuck's *taking* her . . .

Old Woman   i could *kill* for some food

Man   oh is that why you still come

Old Woman (*checks*)   what

Man   for the fare

Old Woman   no no i couldn't care less i mean what's food at my age

Man   so what are you doing here

Old Woman   well it's what me and brian did

Man   each saturday

Old Woman   three o'clock

Man   but brian's not here anymore darling

Old Woman   i know

Man   so you dine alone

Old Woman   well who else is there (*She stares back at* **Man** *longingly.*)

Man   no idea

Old Woman   no no i know he's not here properly of course but i always cut him a slice just in case

Man (*stares at* **Old Woman** *nonplussed*)   in case what

Old Woman   well it was his favourite you see

Man   the salt beef (**Old Woman** *nods confirmingly.*) well you certainly take good care of him mrs cider i mean taking into account what he did

Old Woman   no no it was all *her* fault i told you

Man   busty bertha

Old Woman   besides he took good care of me

Man   did he

Old Woman (*nods*)   left me a nice little nest egg

Man (*his ears prick up*)   really

Old Woman   of course she tried to snatch it for herself but to no avail

Man   snatch what love

Old Woman   well the flat

Man (*his ears prick up*)   the flat (**Old Woman** *nods confirmingly*.) which block

Old Woman   lords view

Man   lords view hey (*He looks impressed.*) which number

Old Woman   sixty three

Man   sixty three (*He nods attentively.*) i see (*He picks up her keys and puts them in his pocket then almost as an afterthought does the same with her purse.*) lovely

Old Woman (*raises her cup*)   cheers

Man   oh yeh *cheers* mrs cider (*He raises his glass and they both sip.*)

The storm grows fiercer outside.

Old Woman   so when did you meet this date of yours

Man   what (**Old Woman** *looks stumped.*) oh last night

Old Woman (*looks surprised*)   where

Man (*nods*)   at a nightclub

Old Woman   and what's her name

Man   her name (**Old Woman** *looks stumped.*) lorraine

Old Woman   oh now *there's* a good old fashioned name

Man   she's a good old fashioned *girl* mrs cider

Old Woman   and where does she live

Man   oh around here

Old Woman (*looks impressed*)   she must be *rich*

Man   well that's what *i* thought

Old Woman   rich bitch from st johns wood hey

Man   precisely

Old Woman   i like it

Man   so do *i* mrs cider believe me

Old Woman   how old is she

Man   well younger than you

Old Woman   what

Man   i mean i'm not *that* fucking desperate (**Old Woman** *chortles loudly.*) hey

Old Woman   so when is she coming about now

Man (*nods*)   she's a bit late

Old Woman   woman's prerogative dear

Man (*frowns and nods concedingly*)   i guess

Old Woman (*nods comprehendingly*)   and that's why you came back

Man   what

Old Woman   after all these years

Man (*nods confirmingly*)   and i don't live near neither

Old Woman   oh where do you

Man   bethnal green

Old Woman (*looks aghast*)   but i thought you was a man of means

Man (*opens his arms*)   disguising it perfectly

Old Woman   well you sure are living in bethnal bloody green

Man   i told her about this place and do you know . . . (*He stares back at* **Old Woman** *enquiringly.*)

Old Woman   what

Man   she never knew it

Old Woman (*gapes at* **Man**)   what

Man   i know

Old Woman   kosher *harrys*

Man   i *know*

Old Woman   but she *lives* around here

Man   i *know* darling i fucking *know* (*they gape at each other*) i said you must know kosher *harrys* darling she said no – i said *surely* – she said no – i said bloody fucking *nora* darling – she said well there's no need to swear – i said no no sorry love i'm just a bit shocked somewhat you know what i mean

Old Woman   i certainly *do*

Man   never mind that mrs cider i'm talking

Old Woman   oh sorry

Man   she said what *is* this place – i said kosher *harrys* – she said yeh yeh kosher fucking *harrys* – now *she* was swearing – after ticking me off – can you *believe* that – but i let it go – i said kosher fucking *harrys* darling is the doyen of all kosher kosher – she said but i've not been there – i said well then love – she said what – i said i must take you – she said you take me – i said sure – sure i said why not – i was being hip – deadpan you see

Old Woman   clearly

Man   she said but i'm not kosher – i said well i can see *that* darling i mean i'm not fucking *blind* . . .

Old Woman   why what does she look like

Man   i said kosher or not darling it doesn't *matter* – harry doesn't *discriminate* i said – she said harry – i said the boss – she said ohh . . .

Old Woman   but harry sold this place years ago

Man   what (*He looks stumped.*) well i know that (**Old Woman** *smiles wryly at* **Man** *who smirks to himself.*) obviously

Old Woman   quite the con man aren't you i dunno what to believe and what *not*

Man   well it depends on the company dunnit darling i mean some people are easy prey

Old Woman   but you spot them well

Man   well they give themselves away

Old Woman   oh so how did them two over there inspire your treachery (*She indicates* **Cabbie** *and* **Waitress** *off stage.*)

Man   who says they did

Old Woman   - well you lied to them about going to spain

Man (*looks stumped*)   no no that was an innocent *blunder* darling

Old Woman   but you don't seem the type

Man   well even *i* have my foibles

Old Woman (*scoffs dismissively*)   no no not you

Man   tell that to *lorraine* love i'll pay for your meal

Old Woman   go on tell me what she looks like

Man   she's black mrs cider

Old Woman (*looks taken aback*)   what

Man   black (**Old Woman***'s face drops and she becomes completely paralysed apart from her face*)   what's the matter love

Old Woman   but you said she was a *blonde*

Man   did i

Old Woman   black blonde is she

Man   well i suppose she *must* be yeh

Old Woman   you mean you dunno

Man   i can't really recall it was *dark* in there

Old Woman   and she's coming here

Man   yeh it's all been arranged

Old Woman   but what will he *do*

Man   who (*He stares nonplussed at* **Old Woman** *then twigs and indicates* **Cabbie** *off stage.*) oh never mind *him* darling he'll cope

Old Woman   no no

Man   never yield to *bullies* mrs cider us two should *know* that more than most

Old Woman (*scoffs*)   *you* should yeh what with *your* history at school but why me

Man   well being a jew

Old Woman (*looks confused*)   and what are you (**Man** *stares at old woman impassively*) you mean you lied (**Man** *stares at* **Old Woman** *impassively*) you fooled me

Man (*looks stumped*)   no no not *you* lovely

Old Woman   ohh

Man (*indicates* **Cabbie** *and* **Waitress** *off stage*)   *them* (**Old Woman** *looks disheartened.*) what's up

Old Woman   i dunno anything about you really other than you used to get taunted perhaps that's why you're so guarded

Man   well you have to be somewhere like this with the likes of him objecting to my date and that

Old Woman   but say she can't eat the food

Man   what

Old Woman   this lorraine person what if she only eats i dunno . . . (*She checks.*)

Man   what

Old Woman   banana fritters (**Man** *stares at* **Old Woman** *nonplussed*.) they don't do them here this is a classy establishment (**Man** *stares at* **Old Woman** *nonplussed*.) black bitch

Man   who is (*He twigs*.) ohh of *course* (*He nods comprehendingly*.) forgive me i forgot (*He gapes at* **Old Woman**.) busty bertha (*He gapes at* **Old Woman**.) black was she (*He gapes at* **Old Woman**.) liked a bit of tan did he your man (**Old Woman**'s *face tenses*.) couldn't show your face i bet amongst your set (**Old Woman** *looks helpless*.) and even when you did was you ostracised (**Old Woman** *looks crestfallen*.) lovely (**Cabbie** *walks on with a huge wet patch around his crotch*) oh here it is

Cabbie   er . . . (*looks all around him*) what is

Man   what happened

Cabbie   well it was all going perfectly to plan mate until . . .

Man   what (*He gapes at* **Cabbie**.) you pissed yourself

Cabbie   what (**Cabbie** *gets a shock as he looks down at his crotch*.) blimey

Old Woman   it musta been the lager it goes right through him

Cabbie   there that explains why she went off me

Old Woman   terrible

Cabbie   russian *pig*

Man   did you follow my tips

Cabbie (*nods*)   to the letter

Old Woman   so was you acting dumb

Cabbie   well as dumb as i *could* missus yeh

Old Woman   and was you being forceful

Cabbie   well i grabbed her a couple of times if that's what you mean

Old Woman   oh so you kept your cool then

Cabbie   what

Man   you didn't come on too strong

Cabbie   no no

Old Woman   and how did she respond

Man   she ridiculed him

Cabbie (*checks*)   what (**Man** *shakes his head to himself disdainfully.*) no no (**Cabbie** *reconsiders.*) although she didn't exactly come to my aid when i had my little mishap that's true

Man   look at her you can see her sniggering (*He indicates* **Russian** *off stage who* **Cabbie** *peers at.*)

Cabbie   where

Man   milking it for all it's worth just like that poppadom does

Cabbie (*checks*)   what

Man   with your son

Cabbie (*looks bemused*)   what are you talking about

Man   rubs his nose in it

Cabbie (*looks bemused*)   does he

Man   sticks the knife in yeh (**Cabbie** *looks bemused.*) smiles to his face

Cabbie   well they're best mates now them two (*He chortles to himself.*) blimey i can't work it out (*He reconsiders.*) still at least it's company for him but what a blooming cross for my lad to *bear* . . .

Man   when really he's torturing him

Cabbie (*checks*)   what

Man   slowly and painfully and in the final throes of his life (*He shakes his head to himself disdainfully.*) despicable

Cabbie   paki cunt

Man   oh don't say that mate

Old Woman   why shouldn't he

Man   well my date mrs cider

Old Woman   what about her (**Man** *turns to face* **Old Woman**.) paki (**Man** *nods confirmingly*.) no (**Old Woman***'s face tenses.*) you said she was black

Man   she is

Old Woman   half black half paki

Cabbie   sorry what was that

Man   oh yeh and half russian

Cabbie (*sticks his finger in his ear and gives it a shake*)   no no i didn't catch that

Old Woman (*yells impatiently and in a strong bethnal green cockney accent which betrays her roots and which remains with her for the rest of the play*)   oh for fuck sake he said *russian*

Cabbie   no (*looks taken aback.*) did you get that missus

Old Woman   well of *course* i did

Cabbie   no no talk to me dear (*walks over towards* **Old Woman** *and gives her a shake.*) she's stuck mate

Man   what

Cabbie   rock solid (*gives* **Old Woman** *another shake but to no avail.*) she won't blooming *budge*

Old Woman   well *do* something you fucking *spastic*

Cabbie   yeh yeh alright missues (*feels his backside and realises his trousers are torn*) oh what's this

Old Woman   what's the matter

Cabbie   hold on a minute missus (*sits on a chair then stands up again holding it tightly against his backside so that his underwear doesn't show*) now let's see what we can do for you darling

Waitress   here we are sir

Cabbie   (*gawps and stands frozen to the spot as waitress walks on without her top but in her bra. She sports a tattoo with Antonio's name. She is holding a tray with everyone's food.*)   blimey

Waitress   (*takes the food off the tray and puts it on the table as if there were nothing unusual*)   the bill sir (*hands **Man** the bill*) it's all there

Man   good good

Waitress   service *not* included

Man   even better

Old Woman   so where is the black bitch

Cabbie   (*nods concurringly*)   paki shit

Waitress   (*looks bemused*)   who are they talking about

Man   my date

Waitress   (*raises her eyebrows*)   oh is she still coming

Old Woman   well of course she is she wouldn't pass up a man like him (*smirks derisively*) *she* should be so lucky

Waitress   no no i thought she may have stood you up sir

Old Woman   she's just a bit *late* that's all

Waitress   oh not too keen on her are they them two i can't say i'm surprised sir (*smiles smugly then checks*) here i never knew she was foreign (**Man** *nods*) black

Man   with a hint of bratislavan

Waitress (*face drops*)   what

Man   just her mother's side mind

Waitress   even *so* sir

Man   her dad's spanish

Waitress (*face drops*)   what (**Waitress** *takes off her spectacles and rubs her eyes and puts them back on again*) here who turned off the lights (*takes off her spectacles and puts them on the table then rubs her eyes again*)

Man   yeh i thought you two might get on i mean i know ho much you like the ol spanish

Waitress (*tenses*)   right that's it bring her in here the spanish cunt (*stumbles around with her arms outstretched trying to get her bearings*) is she here yet

Man (*tucks his napkin into his collar and begins to eat. The others remain silent. Lost in their own mire.* **Man** *enjoys the different pickles and puts salt on his fries etc. The food fills a gaping hole inside him. One that has been there since his school days. He dons the spectacles and studies the bill then scrunches it up and tosses it on the floor. He rises and sticks his hand in* **Cabbie**'s *jacket pocket and pulls out some keys.*)   here where was your cab

Cabbie (*stares back blankly at* **Man** *who dangles the keys in front of him*)   oh outside on the left

Man (*nods and picks up* **Cabbie**'s *taxi badge off the table and puts it around his neck and pats* **Cabbie** *on the back*)   here i hope you filled up the tank you mingy cunt (**Cabbie** *stares blankly at* **Man** *who goes up to* **Waitress**) oh never mind we'll soon see

Cabbie   i tell you what you ain't half a scruffy cunt mate i mean what the fuck is he *wearing* . . .

Waitress   well i dunno

Cabbie (*checks*)   sorry what was that

Waitress   i can't *see* anything

Cabbie   coming out like that (*sneers at* **Man** *disdainfully*) i dunno (**Man** *rises and lifts* **Cabbie***'s jacket off the back of the wheelchair*) you should be *ashamed* (**Man** *puts on the jacket*) i mean look at *us* lot that's what you wanna *aspire* to mate (*nods approvingly*) my wife bought me that you see that's *much* better (**Man** *takes the ear ring off the table and clips it to his ear*) ooh i dunn about that

Man *wraps the remainder of the food in napkins and stuffs them in his pockets. He walks towards the door and steps out but rain falls on his head. He walks back towards* **Old Woman** *and lifts her wig from her head to reveal a bald scalp with a few unsightly tufts of hair sprouting out*

Old Woman   oh has it got drafty

Man *plonks the wig on his head and exits and closes the door behind him.*

Cabbie   that's better

Waitress (*nods concurringly*)   much better

From **Old Woman Man** *has taken her wig and her cardigan and her keys and purse. From* **Waitress** *he has taken her spectacles and an ear ring. From* **Cabbie** *he has taken his taxi badge and his keys and his jacket.*

Old Woman   i tell you what love (*titters to herself*)

Waitress   what

Cabbie   sorry what was that darling

Old Woman   when she *does* come . . .

Waitress   oh yeh

Cabbie   no . . . (*sighs wearily and raises his voice*) can you speak *up* a bit love

Old Woman (*gasps to herself in awe*)   she'll spoil a lovely afternoon

Old Woman *is bald and has no cardigan and is paralysed.*
Waitress *has no shoes on and no spectacles and only one sock and one ear ring and her lipstick is smudged violently across her face and she is in her bra and is blind.* **Cabbie** *is in his vest and is clutching his chair against his backside while he stands and he has a huge wet patch around his crotch and he can't hear for toffee.*

Printed in the USA
CPSIA information can be obtained
at www.ICGtesting.com
LVHW020844171024
794056LV00002B/392